A Handbook of Science Fiction for Teachers
By Elizabeth Calkins/Barry McGhan

TEACHING TOMORROW

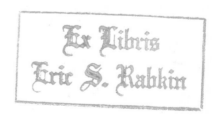

Pflaum / Standard
38 West Fifth Street, Dayton, Ohio 45402

illustration by Lee Burdine

Library of Congress Catalog Card Number 72-83236
© 1972 by Elizabeth Calkins and Barry McGhan
Manufactured in the United States of America
Published by Pflaum/Standard, 38 West Fifth Street,
Dayton, Ohio 45402

ISBN 0-8278-0040-1
10040/3M/S3M-2-773

ACKNOWLEDGMENTS

The following people deserve special mention for their advice and assistance in the preparation of this material: Barbara McGhan for her critical opinions on the prose structure and content, and Harlan McGhan and Howard Devore for their advice on the content of the many lists. We are also indebted to Alexei Panshin and Damon Knight for their recommendations regarding basic science fiction collections (which have appeared in *The Library Journal*), and to Donald Franson for the information contained in his pamphlet *A History of the Hugo, Nebula, and International Fantasy Awards*. We, of course, assume all responsibility for the accuracy of our information; corrections and comments are welcomed.

B.R.M.
E.J.C.

FOREWORD

A few words about this handbook are in order. In part, it is a guide to the important works and practitioners (amateur and professional) in the field of science fiction. We feel that it is only through these works and practitioners that one can come to know the field well. We have, therefore, mostly avoided offering our own opinions about the nature, scope, and value of Sf, other than what is implied in our selections and omissions.

We have also included a discussion of some of our school experiences with the field and offer them, not as a blueprint for other teachers, but rather as examples of things felt and attempted, things which may or may not be appropriate for others.

IV

"It would be gratifying to indulge in idealistic camouflage and proclaim science fiction as an *avant-garde* medium opening the doors on and stimulating the developments of the future, prophesying the fortunes of the human race and sounding tocsins against the social pitfalls that lie ahead. But let's face it: perfect honesty will have to recognize science fiction, and all other forms of literature for that matter, fundamentally on the basis of entertainment value. It is satisfying to know, though, that besides discharging its primary function, science fiction can and does provide these other services in the nature of bonuses. In that respect, the *genre* stands out as the most thorough and most appealing."

—Daniel F. Galouye

(reprinted with permission from *The Double Bill Symposium* copyright 1969 by William C. Mallardi and William L. Bowers)

CONTENTS

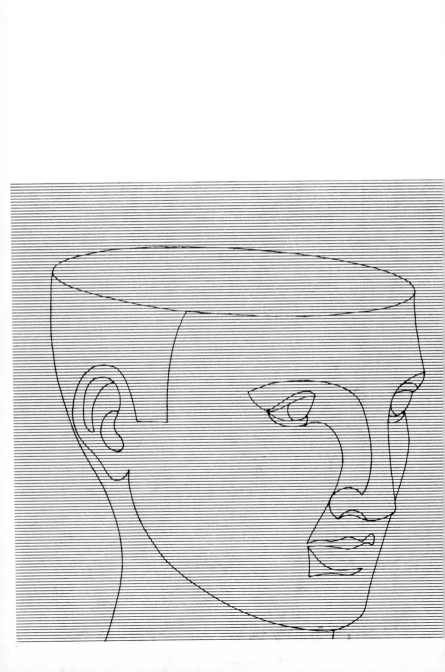

PART ONE

CHANGING CRITERIA FOR COURSES IN HIGH SCHOOL ENGLISH

Few would argue with the traditional goals of most high school English courses. Students were encouraged to improve their reading and writing skills through encounters with examples of the best literature. By this means, their tastes in literature were formed and great ideas of the past were kept alive.

To these ends, materials for high school English courses were selected from a standard group of titles. American Literature included poems by Longfellow, Lowell, Whitman, and Poe; a few short stories; novels, such as *The Red Badge of Courage*, *The Scarlet Letter*, and possibly *Moby Dick*, and the play *Our Town*. English Literature included the "Prologue" to *The Canterbury Tales* and *Julius Caesar*; a few poems by Byron, Shelley, and Keats; *A Tale of Two Cities* and *Silas Marner*, excerpts from *Gulliver's Travels*, and perhaps novels by Jane Austen or Thomas Hardy.

An anthology made everything quite simple because it contained explanations of the social, political, and literary history of each selection. Students used the anthology to "survey" the literature of each country and gain an understanding of its growth and development, including major trends, significant writers, and the great ideas that were produced. Few people asked why certain titles were always taught. What had come to be considered "literature" was somehow mysteriously divided from material that was not. Non-literature was "popular" and did not have to be taught.

Unfortunately, the program did not seem to work. Students were reluctant to read the "greats," and only a few would read an item not specifically assigned. They looked with distaste at standard high school requirements and, once free of them, resolved never to read such books again.

Dissatisfaction with such a traditional program became, in this age of confrontation, more and more openly expressed. Many schools have been sensitive to the discontent of their students and the criticism of the public. New concepts have emerged from attempts to change what happened in the classroom. Some of these concepts are:

1. Survey courses (such as a year's work in American or English Literature) no longer seem so valid. In their place, new courses are being developed to give students an opportunity to study some special fields in depth.

2. Reading materials are being selected in relation to the experience and interests of the student rather than to some arbitrary concept of what constitutes a "classic" which will improve his mind.

3. All students need a series of successful reading experiences to develop the basic skills and attitudes needed so that they will continue to read and explore independently.

4. Changes in public attitudes about what constitutes good taste make it possible to include contemporary selections with more freedom of vocabulary. Also other countries and cultures have produced writing that students need to discover.

5. Learning will be enhanced if the student gains an increased sense of involvement by participating in decision-making about the class. He needs a voice in the reading choices and systems of evaluation.

6. The high school English teacher is no longer the dispenser of wisdom. The teacher's role should be that of organizing the group for discovery, of providing

the materials, and of assisting in identifying valid goals for group achievement.

While all of these pedagogical concepts increase the difficulty of choosing reading selections for high school courses, they also present teachers with new and exciting opportunities.

Science fiction belongs to the new era in English. The public's awareness of the advance of technology, dramatized by such events as moon flights and organ transplants, gives science fiction great currency and relevance. The news media constantly remind us of the future's promises and threats. These reminders make the speculation in science fiction books attractive to young people interested in making a better world. Moreover, since it stems from the popular culture, and is new to the academic world, it is easy for the teacher to adopt a less authoritarian, more student-oriented approach when using it in the classroom.

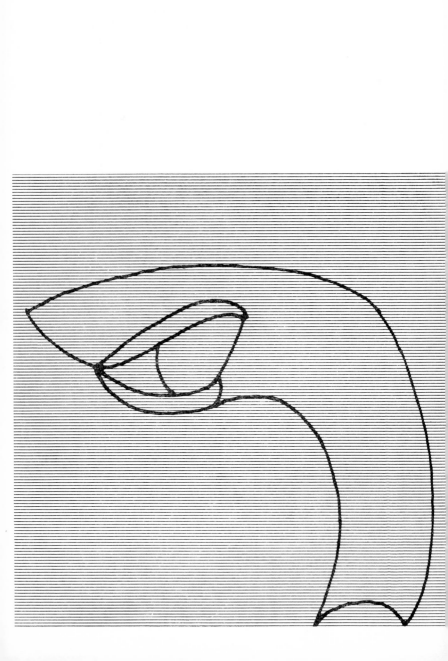

SCIENCE FICTION AND ACADEME

One youngster, on hearing of a proposed high school course in science fiction (hereafter, Sf), asked, "But what is there to teach?" This question really asks, What requires *study* in this field? The question also implies the existence of an attitude that there is no necessity to learn how to read popular writing, or, perhaps, that popular writing is not worthy of serious classroom study. Just what *does* justify using Sf in a high school English program?

The most obvious reason for using Sf in high school hardly needs stating: it provides students with interesting written material through which their skills in reading and writing can be improved.

Another reason for using Sf is that such a course constitutes the study of a genre.[1] This is a traditional approach to the study of literature, although Sf has not been (unlike Gothic novels) an academically recognized genre. Students in a high school course might concern themselves with the definition of this genre and with the relationship between it and other areas of literature.

> One of the obvious values of genre study is precisely the fact that it calls attention to the internal development of literature. . . . Whatever the relations of literature to other realms of value, books are influenced by books; books imitate, parody, transform other books . . .

5

Genre should be conceived . . . as a grouping of literary works based, theoretically, upon both outer form (specific meter or structure) and also upon inner form (attitude, tone, purpose—more crudely, subject and audience).

The Gothic novel is . . . a genre by all the criteria one can invoke for a prose-narrative genre; there is not only a limited and continuous subject-matter or thematics, but there is a stock of devices (descriptive-accessory and narrative, e.g., ruined castles, Roman Catholic horrors, mysterious portraits, secret passageways reached through sliding panels; abductions, immurements, pursuits through lonely forests). (*Theory of Literature,* pp. 231-235)

One example of the efforts that are being made toward the definition of Sf as a genre can be found in a doctoral dissertation by D. N. Samuelson, called *Studies in the Contemporary American and British Science Fiction Novel* (University of Southern California, 1969). Mr. Samuelson says, in part,

As a kind of literature of ideas, science fiction in its 'purer' forms shares the basic assumptions (determinism, empiricism, relativism) and goals (prediction, control, comprehension) of science. Pure science fiction deals with measurable and explainable phenomena (in man as well as in nature), projects or extrapolates contemporary phenomena and ideas into the future, and approximates the form and style of a logical discursive essay.

. . . Science plays an important role: backgrounds tend to be logically extrapolated, orientation tends to be outward in space and forward in time, technological hardware is prominent, the mind and the continuity of intellect are emphasized, and at least one major character represents the 'scientific' features meaningful in terms of ordinary human problems and desires.

Further efforts to identify and analyze the field are needed. For instance, characterization in Sf novels is apt to be flat; most Sf characters are mere stereotypes. This is not necessarily a fault, especially if the "hero" (i.e., the point of interest and identification of the reader) is the plot itself. Perhaps the biggest drawback to the development of an accepted definition is that it is difficult to make the usual judgments of excellence about specific examples of the genre.

Although the preceding paragraphs defend the study of Sf in high school as a genre, such study does not need to be justified as much as it needs to be explained. The need to explain how Sf can be used arises from the fact that, because instruction in Sf has not been part of the academic pattern, it is not very well known. Probably, for many people, monster films and comic books come to mind when the term "science fiction" is mentioned. However, this reputation, as is so often the case with reputations, is inaccurate. A list of books commonly accepted as Sf by devotees of the genre may help to define the classification.

For example, such titles as Mary Shelley's *Frankenstein,* Bram Stoker's *Dracula,* Edward Bellamy's *Looking Backward,* and Eugene Zamaitan's *We,* could be included. We can also include Karel Capek's *War With The Newts,* Lord Dunsany's *The Book of Wonder,* Robert Graves' *Watch the North Wind Rise,* George R. Stewart's *Earth Abides,* Kurt Vonnegut, Jr.'s *Player Piano,* and Gore Vidal's *Messiah.* Of course, the books of H.G. Wells and Jules Verne have acquired their own special fame.

Many of these titles have a "literary" standing and are apt to be recognized by the general reader, or turn up in a college course under one category or another. Many people would name Aldous Huxley's *Brave New World* and George Orwell's *1984* as further examples. Some might also include such books as Jonathan Swift's *Gulliver's Travels* and Lewis Carroll's *Alice in Wonderland.*

There are also other titles which have been difficult to fit into any recognized classification and which, in retrospect, may now be collected under the general heading of Sf. Examples of such books are: Plato's *Timaeus,* Francis Bacon's *New Atlantis,* Tommaso Campanella's *Civitas Solic,* Samuel Butler's *Erewhon,* and Bernard de Mandeville's *Grumbling Hive.*

Although some people feel that the term "speculative fiction" better describes the various kinds of writing usually included in the field, the force of custom is such that the term "science fiction" seems permanently established. But the fact remains that the field is not clearly defined. It can include or exclude any of the works above, either those written before the 1930's (when science fiction developed into a recognizable genre), or ones by contemporary writers who don't usually work within the Sf milieu.

For a high school course, the titles which we later suggest fit into a "contemporary Sf" classification. This classification refers to that body of literature which has been turned out by a relatively small group of writers *who think of themselves* as Sf writers. For the most part, these writers all belong to the Science Fiction Writers Association (SFWA) and regularly publish stories and articles in professional and amateur science fiction magazines. There are, of course, a number of earlier writers, now either dead or retired, who have written stories which also fit into this classification. In a sense, our booklist constitutes a working definition of the field, even though it is neither inclusive nor exclusive.

Added understanding of the value of the field can be gained from another fact: Sf is beginning to receive recognition in the academic world.

Syracuse University has the most serious long-term project in connection with collecting Sf manuscripts and related materials. The George Arents Research Library there has published a catalog of its Sf collection, and the Science Fiction Writers Association has its archives at Syracuse. Harvard's Widener Library also makes a serious effort to collect Sf materials. Courses in Sf are now being offered in many colleges across the country[2] and three doctoral theses in the field have been recently accepted.[3] Sf writers appear with other authors to read and discuss their works (Sf writer Isaac Asimov appeared at Harvard in a series including L.C. Knights, John Updike, and Richard Wilbur). The *Library Journal* and *American Libraries* have carried major articles about Sf by Sf writers Alexei Panshin and James Blish.

Not only do academicians seem more interested in Sf, but Sf devotees are continually developing bibliographic materials which make the field increasingly available for serious study. An *Encyclopedia of Science Fiction and Fantasy* is being prepared by Advent Publishers, with Volume I scheduled for publication in 1972. The Mirage Press offers *The Guide to Science-Fantasy Reference Works,* a bibliography of more than seven hundred reference works on the subject in all languages. Mirage also plans to publish the third edition of an index to science-fantasy publishers, which will include summaries of the contents of books and information about the edition, jacket artists, and pagination. This publisher also offers the *Atlas of Fantasy,* a book of maps of lands and worlds that never were, including unpublished maps drawn by authors from Edgar Rice Burroughs to Andre Norton and Fritz Leiber.

[1]For an excellent extended definition of a literary genre, as well as a discussion of various aspects of genre study, see Rene Wellek and Austin Warren, *The Theory of Literature,* Harcourt Brace and World, Inc.: New York. 3rd ed. 1956. pp. 231-236.

[2]The pamphlet *Science Fiction Comes to College,* compiled by Jack Williamson, lists more than 50 college courses. Williamson's address is Box 761, Portales, N.Mex. 88130.

[3]In addition to Samuelson's thesis mentioned above, we have: Anderson, Ray. *Persuasive Functions of Science-Fiction*: *A Study in the Rhetoric of Science.* (U. of Minn., 1968) and Philmus, Robert. *Into the Unknown*: *The Evolution of Science Fiction in England from Francis Godwin to H.G. Wells.* (U. of Cal. at San Diego, 1968).

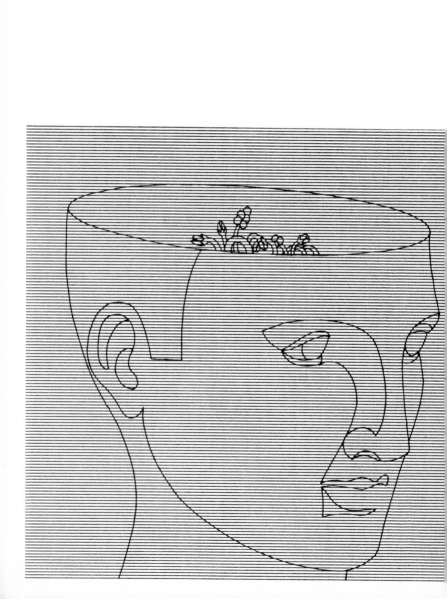

USING SCIENCE FICTION IN THE CLASSROOM

One reason Sf works in the classroom is that students feel the genre belongs to them and not to the teacher. They have encountered ideas about Sf in comic strips, on TV, or in the movies, so that it is a familiar part of the background of many young lives. Classes often include students who have read a great deal of Sf on their own. These students play the role of expert to their peer group. It is a fact of no small importance that the popularity of Sf makes it socially respectable for one male student to discuss it with another, and other students feel a need to read so that they will be as well-informed as their classmates. All these circumstances provide a climate which encourages reading.

The Sf field is specially suited for use in a heterogeneously grouped classroom because of the range of reading levels available. Some books will appeal to relatively unsophisticated readers, while there are difficult and challenging works available as well. (Frank Herbert's *Dune*, for example, is not a book for every student; others respond strongly to it.)

Whatever the reading level, there is apt to be something for each student if the classroom library has a large enough selection of titles available. In the past, high school teachers have pushed students on to other plateaus of learning before they were really ready to make the transition. The result was that many students felt more mystified than enlightened. Reading a great many Sf novels gives them an opportunity for lateral experiences so that they can progress more comfortably at their own rates of learning.

The high school English class has traditionally been the place where students are formally introduced to basic literary forms and elements. Teachers are not surprised to encounter the student who does not really grasp the meaning of such basic terms as "fiction" and "non-fiction." Even the word "novel" is not always in the vocabulary of all students. Such situations arise partly because the students have not had enough reading experiences, and partly because such abstractions about writing are not always introduced until high school.

The Sf novel provides a particularly useful place to begin the study of formal elements. For example, making a list of the main characters of 10 books and listing the dominant qualities of each might demonstrate the flatness of Sf characterization. The story line and the world of the Sf book are often so distinctive that the problem of setting can be readily identified. Since the plot is apt to be rather simple, summaries can reveal elements of suspense and permit students to see how similar many of the plots are.

Because Sf books as a rule are short, it is possible for students to read complete novels quickly and to read a great many of them in a fairly short period of time. Discussion groups can consider the books read by various members. Students can read each other's papers as well as book reviews in standard sources and special Sf publications. In this way, knowledge of a whole field of literature can be acquired. Such knowledge makes it possible for students to arrive at generalizations and to make classifications about an area of literature for themselves.

The range of materials provides many opportunities for the students to begin to develop a sense of literary discrimination, and could even lead the group to develop some criteria for evaluating fiction in general.

The subject matter of the Sf novel is *always* presented in the plot or story line of the book, which is the natural focus of interest for the average high school student.

He likes stories, so his primary response is to the narrative. He is also apt to be optimistic about the future, to be willing to suspend disbelief, and to speculate about the possible directions for the world of the future.

The setting of the Sf novel, or the "world" of the book, is usually the major vehicle for conveying the unique vision of the author. Through discussion of the setting, the students can acquire skills and techniques that will enable them to verbalize concepts about their own world. In fact, Sf writers often *intend* their writing to be critical of sundry aspects of present society.

Sf writers as a group express a sense of responsibility of the present for the future; they also raise a number of interesting questions for students to discuss. Some examples of the themes which have long concerned Sf writers are: overpopulation, ecology, a philosophy of history, the true nature of man, the limitations of man's capabilities to adapt to different conditions of existence, the nature of intelligence, problems in communication (the idea of telepathy fascinates students), systems of morality, eugenic control, and the nature of reality. In Sf, there is a freedom to try out ideas, to explore, and to experiment. The resulting bizarre and extreme elements appeal to the young reader.

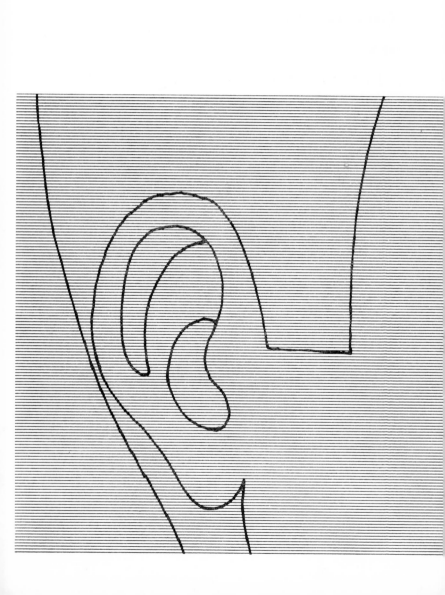

THE ROLE
OF
THE TEACHER

Few English teachers would probably qualify as experts in Sf. This gives them the opportunity to discover a classroom role different from the one to which they are accustomed. With Sf, the teacher needs to inform himself about the field. He should know something of its history, its extent, its organization, and its definition. He can bring materials to the classroom, including class sets of books, and a small classroom library of different titles is essential.

Thus, one important aspect of the role of the teacher is to assemble material. In a sense, he has always provided some material for a class, though often it was merely an anthology. In an Sf course, he will need to use a wide variety of sources: many books, many periodicals, people who have expert knowledge, as well as visual aids that are available.

For instance, the teacher could bring in samples of supporting periodicals, including serious amateur Sf magazines like *Riverside Quarterly* and *Extrapolation*. The amateur publications called "fanzines" should be especially appealing to the students; they are numerous and apt to be devoted to a wide variety of special interests. For special collectors, there are publications that deal with the exchange and sale of books, old magazines, and comic books. These materials provide opportunities for students to correspond with others interested in the field and to develop shared interests. Some Sf authors even find time to reply to letters from their readers.

The teacher can also assemble some critical materials in addition to those that appear in periodicals, so that students have an opportunity to learn what Sf criticism is like. Perhaps a few issues of the *Library Journal* with its reviews would serve as samples of how to write short summaries. Audio-visual aids[4], such as the movie *Story of a Writer*[5] with Sf author Ray Bradbury, can be used. TV also provides a constant source of Sf movies which can be compared and contrasted with printed Sf material. Finally, the teacher can bring in other Sf buffs from the faculty or the community to talk with the students about their special interests. Some Sf authors may be willing to come to talk with interested groups.

In addition to assembling class resources, the teacher is also responsible for providing a framework in which the group can work successfully together. This means establishing a schedule, defining goals, creating a work pattern, and dealing with the matter of student evaluation. These concerns can be discussed with students, possibly in small groups from various interest areas. While the teacher initiates such discussions, the students' decisions must carry some weight so that they feel a stake in the project, thus increasing their willingness to participate in class work.

In regard to the thorny problem of evaluating progress, perhaps the entire group can agree on empirical measures for individuals, and for the group as a whole (e.g., the number of books read and/or the number of papers written; there must also be some mutually acceptable way of assessing quality).

A week's schedule could provide several days for discussion, at least one day in which the class is divided into small groups, and at least one day in which one of these groups presents material for the entire class. Another day in class could be set aside for group reading of papers. This could mean that, in a group of five, all five would read each other's papers. After discussion, the group would arrive at a grade for each of the papers.

Depending upon the flexibility in a school, other possibilities for organization exist. The entire group may not really need to meet for the entire class hour every day. If special scheduling is possible, alternating days of formal presentations and days of small group or individual work could prove successful. Even in a school which schedules classes every day for a specific time, it is still possible to work out variations in the day's plans.

There is some value in having the whole class read the same book, with small sections of the class making presentations on various aspects of it, e.g., plot, characterization, or setting. Or perhaps several books could be read by different groups in the class and then reported on for general discussion. Students often do not get involved in the ideas of a book without a discussion that allows a variety of reactions to emerge. Without discussion, some students do not even know that such reactions are an essential part of reading. They may think that reading is just looking at the page. They may even know quite a lot about what the words say, but they often will not consider the implications of the words until they talk about the material in a group situation. They then have a better idea of what to look for in the next book.

Since writing is a necessary aspect of English courses, the instructor can also provide a style sheet for acceptable usage. If the class wants to design its own style sheet, so much the better. Successful writing is partly a matter of conforming to a set of accepted practices, but if students rebel, arrangements can be made for some papers to be evaluated on a basis that deemphasizes the formal aspect of writing.

A considerable degree of student involvement in evaluation should be sought. It increases morale and interest and gives students a chance to begin to exercise their critical judgment. In keeping with this principle, writing should be produced for the peer group. If papers are corrected by members of the class (under detailed guidelines), using criteria they have developed, they will learn how to translate their abstract criteria into useful, practical means of evaluation.

Written evaluations by students give them practice in

putting their thoughts on paper and also provide specific feedback to the person whose work is being evaluated. They all want to begin by saying, "It's a good paper," but they usually have a good deal to learn about what makes a paper good, and why. Being required to articulate their own sense of value is the best possible training they can get for improvement in writing. The process of public evaluation of papers tends to give students added cause for careful writing. Inadequate work can no longer be hidden in a pile of papers seen only by the teacher.

In conclusion, we would like to say that, though the techniques discussed in this section could probably be used successfully in areas other than Sf, we think teaching Sf necessitates their use.

Throughout this essay we have explained why we think Sf should have a high place in the English curriculum. We hope that the reader, if not absolutely convinced that it should have a place, is at least more receptive to the idea than before.

[4]Sf writer and teacher James Gunn has produced a series of more than six films on Sf. The series is called "The Literature of Science Fiction." More information can be obtained from: Audio Visual Center, Bailey Hall, U. of Kansas, Lawrence, Kan., 66044.

[5]For more information write: Sterling Educational Films, 241 E. 34th St., New York, N. Y. 10016.

STUDY GUIDES

The following material offers suggestions for papers related to general developments in two stories, *The Puppet Masters* (No. 85 in "Recommended Novels") and *The Space Merchants* (No. 103 in "Recommended Novels"). Suggestions are also included for small group activities centered on literary concepts as they appear in each story.

The decision to use one book with a whole class, or many different books with individuals or small groups, or to work out some combination of these organizational patterns, should be made by each teacher for himself.

THE PUPPET MASTERS

Some suggestions for papers:

1. The slugs: a complete account of their appearance, methods of communication and propagation, their techniques of take over, and the geographical areas they finally controlled.

2. Provide an account of the series of plans that the government used in its effort to repel the slugs. Deal with the satire involving increased nudity as the plans escalate.

3. Why does the author have Sam undergo not one but two experiences of being taken over by the slugs? This paper should include a brief account of each of

the experiences and then an explanation of the significance of what happens to the captive in relation to the theme of the book.

4. An account of Sam's relationship with his father and his wife as a basis for the projection of his moral code. Why is this sort of moral code a necessity for this particular discussion of the attack on freedom?

5. The relationship between Sam and the Old Man (one of the standard Heinlein "wise old man-young protege" designs) as a prototype for the development of the hero-leader.

Suggestions for small group activities:

1. Satire   One group might collect and present to the class examples of satire in the novel. After the satire has been identified, there are a number of areas for discussion. For instance, does Heinlein's ridicule of Congress mean he rejects representative government? What is the usual purpose of satire? How about the behavior of special interest groups when it was required that people shed more and more of their clothing? The simplistic solution (that is, undressing) is a further topic for discussion.

2. Symbol   What is achieved by having the slugs with their loathsome physical characteristics operate as a symbol for spiritual captivity? Compare this treatment of the loss of liberty with others as shown in such books as *Animal Farm, 1984,* and *Brave New World.* Collect further examples about the results of the loss of liberty.

Does Heinlein provide enough clues to exactly identify the concept that the slugs are supposed to represent? Is he attacking merely the political concept of the totalitarian government? What other limitations operate to circumscribe the freedom of the individual? (Ignorance, selfishness, immaturity, etc.)

3. Theme   Liberty—the theme of the novel—appeals to many students as a topic for discussion, but the tendency is to emotionalize and generalize. A series of discussions might be planned with small groups of students as leaders. Each group could undertake some definition of a particular area of liberty. Each could present specific historical documentation about that phase. (The general article in the *Encyclopaedia Britannica* is a good place to start. Perhaps it would be possible to borrow a set of American history books from the history department for further reading. Some key information could then be factually presented. For example: the Mayflower Covenant, Rousseau's natural rights and the social contract, Samuel Adams' *Declaration of the Rights of Man,* the First Continental Congress' *Declaration of Rights and Liberties,* the Declaration of Independence, Tom Paine's *Rights of Man.*

Groups could be specifically assigned:
    civil liberty
    moral liberty or freedom of the will
    political liberty
    economic liberty
    academic freedom

THE SPACE MERCHANTS

Some suggestions for papers:

1. Fowler Schocken, his view of the world, and why his failure to believe Mitch's story about Chlorella and

the Consies led to his death. This topic is an opportunity to present the ad agency's view of the world and to emphasize its system of values.

2. Kathy's reasons for refusing to complete the year's marriage contract with Mitch. This topic is an opportunity to organize and present the Consie view of the world.

3. The re-education of Mitch is the basis for the plot. Since this is so, why did the plot have to include a situation in which Mitch personally encountered the head of the Taunton agency?

Suggestions for small group activities:

1. Extrapolation. The group defines the term for the class, using examples from math, history, and as many fields as possible. The members of the group present as much data as they can identify from the novel to show how the writer has employed the technique. They may then wish to use the same approach to speculate on the future development of certain contemporary trends.

2. Satire. Satire is not always an easy concept for high school students. If a number of examples from the text could be presented by the group, the rest of the class may then recognize the common elements and develop their own definition. Much of the book's criticism of social trends is managed in this way. For instance, the life of the Chlorella workers, the attitudes of Hester's "good" family, public entertainment as a soporific.

3. Analogy. To what purpose does the author establish the parallels between Consies and Commies? For instance, the cell

organization, secrecy, ideology rejected by the common man.

4. Allusion. Richness in the texture of the novel is lost on students if they do not follow frequent allusions. On the other hand, it is deadly for the instructor to identify each one along the way. However, a small group of students who make this topic their choice may be able to present information to the class in an acceptable way.

For instance: Machiavellian, p. 27

Cartier for flowers, p. 27

F. D. R. Memorial, p. 19

Moloch, p. 34

Keats, S w i n b u r n e, great lyricists, p. 38

Victor Herbert's *Toyland,* p. 47

Labor F r e i g h t e r *Thomas R. Malthus,* p. 60

Galton's whistle, p. 80

Brinks, p. 102

Gilles de Rais, p. 102

a fat Napoleon at Elba, p. 140

5. Theme. A. The literal political control of the world by two major advertising agencies representing a rigid materialistic ethic poses the question, Are we now in fact so completely manipulated by advertising? If so, how can individuals escape such a pervasive influence?

(1) Vance Packard's books would provide a starting

point for those who are concerned with exploring modern practices and theories of advertising.

(2) Jack O'Shea boasts that he never reads the ads, and he therefore assumes that he escapes their i n fl u e n c e. Mitch points out the fallacy of this view. A small group might like to undertake an experiment with brand names to discover the range of reactions actually obtained in the class.

(3) A practical group might want to make a collection of ads from radio, TV, newspapers, and magazines to identify the current trends in special advertising appeal.

B. Ecology, the hero, may attract students. The history of the movement and some of the major organizations involved in promoting it would make useful material to present. Statistics on population growth, decrease in natural resources, and interaction of environmental changes are some possible topics for exploration.

CASE
STUDIES

The following case studies stem from our school experiences with Sf. They illustrate some of the things that can and do happen easily in an Sf class, things which are unfortunately all too rare in many ordinary courses.

MIKE

Mike's soft blond hair was conservatively cut and he dressed inconspicuously. His posture said pretty clearly that he had existed through nearly twelve years of school without finding anything that interested him.

He was around for quite a while before I discovered anything about him other than that he habitually produced the weirdest spelling patterns I had encountered in twenty-five years of teaching. He'd read a bit of science fiction here and there, but he had a special passion for one particular series—Kenneth Robson's "Doc Savage" stories. Once, he brought the complete set of more than thirty books to class in an old zipper bag.

Mike never did very well with the general readings, and I don't think his writing or spelling improved much either, even though we worked on them. His knowledge of the field of science fiction may or may not have been extended by the heated group discussions. But he did learn about Doc Savage, and the paper he wrote on the series obviously meant a great deal to him.

His interest motivated him to do further writing. He wrote to the author's widow and received a response.

He wrote to the publishers of the series and asked them to send him additional copies of each of the books because he expected them to become collector's items. He wrote to the artists who had done the illustrations in the early editions. He began to discover a good deal about the early pulp magazines in which the series was first published. He also wrote to business firms that deal in old magazines, books, and comics.

Overall, Mike's skills with language didn't increase much. But because of his inner motivation, his experiences with language were considerably greater than they would have been in many English classes, and we all benefited from his research.

DAVE

Dave was a careless, inattentive student in class. He was not concerned about academic competition and had not bothered to acquire skills for it. His attendance was good and he scarcely missed a day except for a week during hunting season. He came to school, sat in his seat, caused no trouble, and went home. I found it hard to imagine what school meant to such a person.

Now and then I would see him reading a paperback science fiction book during homeroom. Eventually, I discovered that he had a considerable collection of books which he had taken over from his father. He talked more about the collection than about individual titles—apparently the records of three or four hundred books, kept on individual cards, had some special significance for him. He eventually enrolled in the science fiction course. At first, I felt that he regularly missed the point of the books he was reading. One day he brought in Jack London's *Before Adam,* a book I didn't know. When he had finished it, he loaned it to me, and later we had a couple of conversations about it.

I can't see that Dave's knowledge of Sf made much difference in his school career. But when we met, we had something to talk about that, unlike *A Tale of Two Cities,* was fun for both of us.

ED

Ed was the kind of tall, dark kid with a poor complexion who brought the adjective "saturnine" to mind. He spoke so softly in class that practically no one heard him. When we were struggling to get a bridge group going, he patiently helped a blind student, to whom the spatial problems of a card game were a challenge.

His writing was a constant effort to use satire or inversion of some kind, but his technique generally didn't come off. He saw the themes in Sf stories and did not forget them or the plots. He remarked once that one book was a direct steal from another he'd read. His comments about his reading were often brief, but all of them indicated a critical intelligence at work.

A year after he was in my class he came around after school and asked to borrow Frank Herbert's *Dune*, saying that he couldn't imagine why he hadn't read it while he was in the class. In a few days, he brought it back. He was as enthusiastic about it as I had been. A couple of weeks later I saw him in the hall and he told me not to bother with the sequel to *Dune*, that Herbert had said it all in the first book. Obviously, Ed's interest in reading this kind of material lasted longer than the period of formal class instruction.

ANN

Occasionally, students with special qualities come into one's classroom and make it appear that there is some good in the world after all. Ann was such a student, a dark and attractive girl, neither forward nor shy, ladylike without being affected. A truly lovely child.

She particularly liked Ursula LeGuin's award-winning novel *The Left Hand of Darkness* and, as one of the class activities, wrote the author a letter. Mrs. LeGuin replied with several pages of straightforward discussion of the content and ideas about which Ann had inquired. The girl was naturally delighted—and so was I. It is very exciting when a student can have that kind of exchange with an author about a book, and because of the considerable amount of interaction between fans and Sf writers, such exchanges are not unusual.

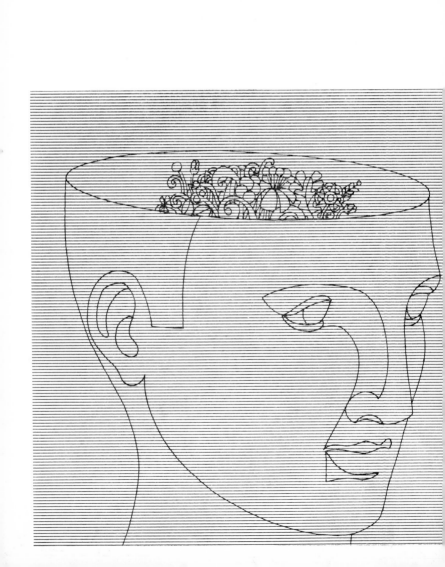

PART TWO

LISTS

The following 12 lists comprise a guide to who and what are important in the field of science fiction. Most of the recommended material can be obtained by mail from the addresses provided. We recognize that valid substitutions can probably be made for some items on these lists, but this is always the case when recommendations are based on opinion. We stand by our choices as being mostly correct. Also, we would like to affirm that, although some people may profit from having their names listed here, all of them are listed on *our* initiative and without collusion.

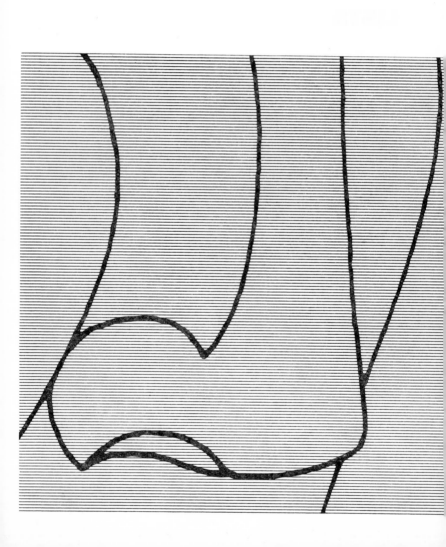

BOOK
DEALERS

1. Science Fiction Sales. Howard DeVore, 4705 Weddel, Dearborn, Michigan 48125.
2. *F and Sf* Book Co. Richard Witter, Box 415, Staten Island, New York 10302.

   Both of the parties above run a mail-catalog business. They deal almost exclusively in the field of science fiction and fantasy, and carry a wide range of new and used hardcover and paperback books, as well as a large number of magazines. They can provide most of the materials recommended in the other lists.

3. *The Fantasy Collector.* Camille Cazedessus, Jr., Box 550, Evergreen, Colorado 80439.

   This publication, now a special section of a fanzine called *ERB-dom,* is a collection of advertisements placed by various people interested in selling such things as books, magazines, fanzines, comics, artwork, novelties, and gadgets.

BOOK PUBLISHERS

The publishers listed below seem to give more attention to the field of science fiction than do most others. When writing for information, address letter to "Science Fiction Editor."

Most science fiction is sold in paperback rather than in hardcover. The publishers in this list, with the exception of Doubleday, concentrate on paperback sales for most of their titles.

1. Ace Publishing Corp., 1120 Avenue of the Americas, New York, New York 10036.
   Ace is almost certainly the leading publisher of science fiction by volume. It publishes about as much as all others combined.

2. Advent Publishers, Box 0228, Chicago, Illinois 60690.
   This small publishing house specializes in science fiction material of a critical or bibliographic nature.

3. Avon Books, 959 Eighth Ave., New York, New York 10019.

4. Ballantine Books, Inc., 101 Fifth Ave., New York, New York 10003.
   This company probably ranks number two in quantity of science fiction published. It was named "Best Publisher" at the 1965 World Science Fiction Convention.

5. Berkley Publishing Corp., 200 Madison Ave., New York, New York 10016.

6. Doubleday & Company, Inc., Garden City, New York 11530.
   This company is the leading *hardcover* publisher of science fiction. It also runs the Science Fiction Book Club, although selections are not restricted to Doubleday printings.

7. Lancer Books, Inc., 1560 Broadway, New York, New York 10036.

8. Pyramid Publications, Inc., 444 Madison Ave., New York, New York 10022.

PROFESSIONAL MAGAZINES

Professional Sf magazines (called "prozines") are digest-sized magazines sold on newsstands and by subscription. These magazines are usually published by companies which also publish other kinds of special and general interest periodicals. As can be seen from the addresses, one company may even publish more than one science fiction magazine.

Although the prozines are intended to be profitable operations, it has often been the case that they barely manage to cover expenses, and many have enjoyed only a brief life-span. The ones listed here are the best and hardiest of the bunch. Address inquiries to "The Editor."

1. *Amazing*, Ultimate Publishing Co., Box 7, Oakland Gardens, Flushing, New York 11364.

2. *Analog Science Fiction—Science Fact,* 420 Lexington Ave., New York, New York 10017.
   This prozine is the most venerable of those listed here. Its former editor, the late John W. Campbell, Jr., held that position for more than 30 years. He is often credited with giving science fiction its modern form through his editorial supervision of writers who have become prominent in the field.

3. *Fantastic.* Same as *Amazing*.

4. *Galaxy,* 421 Hudson St., New York, New York 10014.
   Analog, Fantasy and Science Fiction, and *Galaxy* are probably the three best known prozines.

5. *The Magazine of Fantasy and Science Fiction,* 347 E. 53rd St., New York, New York 10022.
   This prozine has the most "literary" image. It's a recent winner of Hugo awards at the annual World Science Fiction Convention.

6. *Worlds of IF,* Same as *Galaxy.*
   If has won three Hugos for "Best Prozine" since 1966.

AMATEUR PUBLICATIONS

The creation and publication of amateur Sf magazines (called "fanzines") consume a great deal of the time, energy, and money of many of the more avid science fiction readers. Although most fanzines cost their publishers more than sales bring in, they continue to spew out of basement ditto machines, Mimeographs, and offset presses in bewildering numbers. Most often, a publication appears on the scene for a while and then disappears just as suddenly, when the publisher/editor runs out of money, time, things to say, or whatever.

The contents of these little magazines (some of which are lavishly done, with printed copy, art work, and photos) include articles about authors and their works, debates about trends within the field, extensive letter columns, news items, stories, poetry, and drawings. Many professional writers saw their first work printed in a fanzine. They often contribute articles and letters-to-the-editor to the more widely read fanzines (a wide readership might include as many as 500 or 600 subscribers). Most of the ones listed below have been around for a long time (as fanzines go), and give promise to stay around for awhile yet.

1. *Amra,* Box 8243, Philadelphia, Pennsylvania 19101. This fanzine is considered *the* magazine for those interested in "sword and sorcery" type fantasy.

2. *Extrapolation,* College of Wooster, Thomas D. Clareson, Editor, Box 2515, Wooster, Ohio 44691.

This semi-annual publication is not really a fanzine. It is the official publication of the Modern Language Association's Seminar on Science Fiction.

3. *Locus*, Charlie Brown, 2078 Anthony Avenue, Bronx, New York 10457.
   This more-or-less biweekly fanzine carries a considerable amount of information about people and events, publishing activities, recent book and fanzine reviews.

4. *Luna Monthly,* Ann Dietz, 655 Orchard St., Oradell, New Jersey 07649.
   This printed fanzine contains articles, reviews, and notices of current events.

5. *Riverside Quarterly,* Leland Sapiro, Box 40, University Station, Regina, Saskatchewan, Canada.
   This fanzine usually includes articles by pros as well as fans, and all have a decidedly academic flavor. Included is an extensive letter column.

6. *Yandro,* Robert Coulson, Rt. 3, Hartford City, Indiana 47348.
   One of the longest running of the amateur magazines.

SCIENCE FICTION CONVENTIONS

A major preoccupation of dedicated Sf fans is the Sf convention. The conventions can be formal or informal. A typical program might include panel discussions, question and answer sessions, lectures, debates, movie programs, fashion shows, a costume ball, meet-the-pros parties, art shows, auctions of artwork, manuscripts, rare books, etc., book and magazine dealer displays, informal parties.

The World Science Fiction Convention is held on Labor Day weekend in various locales around the country and the world. The location is voted on each year (i.e., this year's convention votes on the next site). The site rotates through zones, viz., West Coast, Midwest, East, Overseas, etc. Recent sites have been Cleveland (1966), New York (1967), Oakland (1968), St. Louis (1969), Heidelberg (1970), and Boston (1971).

In addition to the world convention, a number of regional conventions are held each year. More regional conventions are held than appear in this list. The ones listed are the ones that seem to be firmly entrenched and likely to continue. The organizers of the various conventions vary from year to year, and so names and addresses are difficult to list. However, the names and locations of these events are fairly permanent, and the fanzines carry specific details for each convention as it comes up.

    Boskone—Boston in March
    Disclave—Washington, D.C. in May

Lunacon—New York in April
Midwestcon—Cincinnati in June
Philcon—Philadelphia in November
Westercon—California in July

A relatively new convention deserves special mention. The Secondary Universe Convention (called Secon) "aims at a maximum of interaction, conceptually and personally, among serious professionals in Sf and the other arts, imaginative academics, critics and scientists" to quote from a recent brochure. Secon is held in the fall at various locations and is well advertised in the fanzines.

SCIENCE FICTION ORGANIZATIONS

The National Fantasy Fan Federation, c/o Janie Lamb, Rt. 1, Box 3664, Heiskell, Tenn. 37754.

The NFFF is a kind of umbrella organization, composed of a number of "bureaus" through which science fiction fans engage in certain activities: amateur magazine publishers get help and advice and exchange ideas and materials; tapes of interviews, radio programs, television programs, etc. are disseminated; a lending library is operated; buyers and sellers are brought together; and a number of other functions are performed. By joining NFFF one can get a fairly good idea of what science fiction fandom is like.

Science Fiction Writers of America, Address varies yearly with the election of the Secretary-Treasurer (see *Encyclopedia of Associations*).

The SFWA was formed by Sf writers for the protection of their financial and professional interests. Membership is restricted to writers, but the organization is interested in advancing the status of the field and may provide things like lists of writers who are willing to speak to groups.

Science Fiction Research Association, Thomas D. Clareson, Executive Committee Chairman, Box 3186, College of Wooster, Wooster, Ohio 44691.

This organization is barely out of the talking stage. The purpose is to bring together people interested in the academic aspects of science fiction.

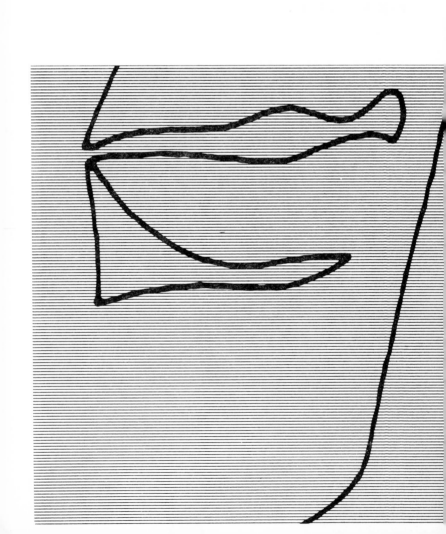

SCIENCE FICTION MOTION PICTURES

In most cases, Sf films are simply horror films in disguise. Many of them, made during the heyday of Sf films in the early fifties, are incredibly bad. In our opinion, they are one reason the field of Sf literature has such a poor image in the eyes of the academic world and the general public. Although there is generally little connection between Sf writing and Sf movies, there is *some* connection. The list below represents a group of films which are above average for the genre and which, for the most part, have some connection with the field of Sf literature.

1. *Charly* (1968). Based on *Flowers for Algernon* by Daniel Keyes.

2. *Day of the Triffids* (1963). Based on the book of the same name by John Wyndham.

3. *The Day the Earth Stood Still* (1951). Based on short story "Farewell to the Master" by Harry Bates.

4. *Destination Moon* (1950). Loosely based on *Rocketship Galileo* by Robert Heinlein, who also worked on the screenplay.

5. *Fahrenheit 451* (1966). Based on the book of the same name by Ray Bradbury.

6. *Fail Safe* (1963). Based on the book of the same name by E. Burdick and J. Wheeler.

7. *Fantastic Voyage* (1966). Book of the same name written from screenplay by Isaac Asimov.

8. *Forbidden Planet* (1956). Book of same name written from screenplay by W. J. Stuart.

9. *1984* (1955). Based on the book of the same name by George Orwell.

10. *On the Beach* (1959). Based on the book of the same name by Nevil Shute.

11. *Panic in the Year Zero* (1962).

12. *The People* (1972). Based on some of the stories of Zenna Henderson.

13. *The Power* (1968). Based on the book of the same name by Frank Robinson.

14. *The Tenth Victim* (1965). Based on the short story "The Seventh Victim" by Robert Sheckley.

15. *Them* (1954).

16. *2001: A Space Odyssey* (1968). Script written by Stanley Kubrick and Arthur C. Clarke from a story by Clarke. Book written from script by Clarke.

17. *War of the Worlds* (1953). Based on the book of the same name by H. G. Wells.

SCIENCE
FICTION
FOR GIRLS

Although many people would probably agree that female readers, writers, and story characters are in short supply in Sf, few would agree on the reasons for the shortage and the rightness or wrongness of it.

Let it suffice to say that, when Sf is a formal part of a school program, it seems desirable to take steps to correct this imbalance. One measure that can be taken is to try to "sell" Sf to girls by introducing them to books which have particular feminine appeal. (An obvious example of such a story would be one with a heroine rather than a hero.)

The list below is a first try at identifying Sf books and stories that might appeal especially to girls. Some fantasy material has been included. Books are listed without regard to suitability for high school use insofar as the treatment of so-called "adult" interests are concerned. Asterisks indicate that a title is available in paperback.

1. Ashwell, Pauline, "Unwillingly to School."

2. Asimov, Isaac, "Susan Calvin" robot stories, "Playmate," *Second Foundation.**

3. Bester, Alfred, *The Stars My Destination.**

4. Blish, James, *Titan's Daughter,** *A Case of Conscience.**

5. Brackett, Leigh, *The Long Tomorrow.**

6. Bradbury, Ray, *The Martian Chronicles.**

7. Brown, Rosel George, (*Galactic*) *Sibyl Sue Blue.**

8. Brunner, John, *Quicksand.**

9. Clement, Hal, *Mission of Gravity,** *Needle,** *Iceworld.**

10. Compton, D. G., *Synthajoy.**

11. DeCamp, L. Sprague, *Rogue Queen,** "Enchanter" stories, "Zei" stories.

12. Del Rey, Lester, "Helen O'Lay," other sentimental stories.

13. Farmer, Philip Jose, *The Lovers.**

14. Harness, Charles, *The Rose.**

15. Heinlein, Robert A., *Podkayne of Mars,** *Door Into Summer,** *Have Space Suit—Will Travel.**

16. Henderson, Zenna, "The People" stories.

17. Hoyle, Fred, *A for Andromeda.**

18. Jackson, Shirley, *The Haunting of Hill House,** "The Lottery."

19. Jones, D. F., *Implosion.*

20. Keyes, Daniel, *Flowers for Algernon.**

21. Leiber, Fritz, *The Big Time,** *Conjure Wife.**

22. L'Engle, Madeleine, *A Wrinkle in Time.*

23. Lewis, C. S. *Perelandra,** et. al.

24. McCaffrey, Anne, *Dragonflight.**

25. MacDonald, John D., *The Girl, the Gold Watch, and Everything.**

26. Merril, Judith, *Shadow on the Hearth,* "Only a Mother."

27. Miller, Walter M., *A Canticle for Leibowitz.**

28. Norton, Andre, *The Year of the Unicorn,* Ordeal in Otherwhere,* Key Out of Time,* The Sorceress of the Witch World.**

29. Pangborn, Edgar, *The Judgment of Eve,* A Mirror for Observers.**

30. Phillips, Mark, *Brain Twister,* The Impossibles,* Super Mind.**

31. Piper, H. B., *Little Fuzzy,* The Other Human Race.**

32. Russ, Joanna, *Picnic in Paradise.**

33. Schmitz, James H., *The Witches of Karres,* The Demon Breed,* The Universe against Her.**

34. Shaw, Bob, "Light of Other Days."

35. Shiras, Walter, *Children of the Atom.**

36. Silverberg, Robert, *Thorns.**

37. Simak, Clifford. Stories with pastoral quality.

38. Stewart, George, *Earth Abides.**

39. Sturgeon, Theodore, *More Than Human.**

40. Swann, Thomas Burnett, *Day of the Minotaur,* The Weirwoods,* Moondust,* The Dolphin and the Deep.**

41. Tolkien, J.R., *Lord of the Rings** (trilogy), et. al.

42. Vercor, J., *Sylva.**

43. Vonnegut, Kurt, Jr., *The Sirens of Titan.**

44. Wilson, Richard, "Mother of the World."

45. Wyndham, John, *Re-Birth.**

46. Zelazny, Roger, *Dream Master,** "A Rose for Ecclesiastes," "The Keys to December."

CRITICAL WORKS

1. Amis, Kingsley. *New Maps of Hell: A Survey of Science Fiction.** New York: Harcourt, Brace and Co. 1960.
   Thorough analysis of the field by an "outside" critic.

2. Atheling, William, Jr. *The Issue at Hand.** Chicago: Advent Publishers. 1964. (2nd Ed. 1967).
   Review and discussion of science fiction magazines of the fifties and early sixties. Atheling is a pseudonym of writer James Blish. A sequel, *More Issues at Hand,* has recently been released.

3. Clareson, Thomas D., ed. *SF: The Other Side of Realism.* Bowling Green: Bowling Green University Popular Press. 1971.
   Twenty-five essays by outstanding international scholars.

4. Davenport, Basil, ed. *The Science Fiction Novel: Imagination and Social Criticism,** Chicago: Advent Publishers. 1959.
   This book is a collection of four essays by writers Heinlein, Kornbluth, Bester, and Bloch based on lectures they gave at the University of Chicago.

5. Franklin, H. Bruce. *Future Perfect: American Science Fiction of the Nineteenth Century.* New York: Oxford University Press. 1966.

6. Knight, Damon. *In Search of Wonder.** Chicago: Ad-

vent Publishers. 1967, 2nd ed.
A collection of revised versions of reviews written while Knight was a book reviewer for various science fiction magazines.

7. Lundwall, Sam J. *Science Fiction: What It's All About.** New York: Ace Books. 1971.

8. Moskowitz, Sam. *Explorers of the Infinite.** New York: World Publishing Co. 1963.
A survey of the field up to about the thirties.

9. Moskowitz, Sam. *Seekers of Tomorrow.** Cleveland and New York: World Publishing Co. 1966.
A continuation of the survey begun in the preceding volume. This volume covers the "big" names of the modern period, up to about the beginning of the sixties. Ballantine Publishers has printed a paperback copy of this work.

10. Wollheim, Donald A. *The Universe Makers: Science Fiction Today.* New York: Harper and Row. 1971.

SCIENCE FICTION INDEXES

The titles are self-explanatory. A number of other indexes have also been compiled, but most are out of print and virtually unobtainable. This kind of reference work is usually the product of long hours of hard work by a dedicated science fiction fan. The field is fortunate to have such people, because science fiction is mostly excluded from standard library indexes.

1. Cole, Walter. *A Checklist of Science Fiction Anthologies*. Brooklyn: W.R. Cole. 1964.

2. Day, Bradford. *The Checklist of Fantastic Literature in Paperbound Books*. Denver, New York: Science Fiction and Fantasy Publishers. 1965.

3. Day, Donald. *Index to the Science Fiction Magazines: 1926-1950*. Portland, Oregon: Perri Press. 1952.

4. Strauss, Erwin. *The MIT Science Fiction Society's Index to the SF Magazines: 1951-1965*. Cambridge, Mass.: MIT Science Fiction Society. 1966. (Supplements are available for 1966, 1967, 1968, 1969.)

5. Viggiano, Michael and Franson, Donald. *Science Fiction Title Changes*. The National Fantasy Fan Federation. 1965.

6. Tuck, Donald. *A Handbook of Science Fiction and Fantasy*. 2nd ed. 2 vols. Hobart, Tasmania: Tuck. 1959. (May soon be reprinted by Advent Publishers.)

RECOMMENDED NOVELS

In recent years, the focus of Sf writing has shifted away from short stories toward novels. For the most part these novels tend to be relatively brief, and it is possible to read many of them during the course of a semester. Because of these facts, and because we believe that students should have many lateral reading experiences, we decided that our main list of recommended readings should be a list of novels.

Having made that decision, we then had to decide which novels to include. We have listed our selection criteria below. Even when our final choices were made we were not entirely happy with the list. Consequently we decided to include a supplementary list of worthwhile material that did not fit our main category, but which gives a more complete view of the field.

As a final hedge, we note that an annotation for a book may not always do justice to the story. Reading condensed reviews of books is like looking at people from a distance—it's hard to see the differences. The reviews in our main list should be taken only as rough indicators of the nature of the story, and most similarities are only apparent ones.

Selection criteria:

The list includes novels suitable to different levels of reading interests and abilities of high school students.

The list reflects an emphasis on including as many authors as possible (without sacrificing quality for dispersion).

The books belong to what is generally considered the modern era of Sf—1938 to the present.

The books have received some popular or critical approval apart from our own. Nearly all books nominated for awards[1] are included. Also included are books which have appeared on lists recommended for basic collections, or on "most popular" lists.

Writers with established reputations outside the field of science fiction, or books with widespread acceptance (e.g., Robert Graves in the former case, *Brave New World* in the latter), are generally not included.

The list is alphabetized by author(s). Other information in addition to the annotations is included wherever pertinent. An asterisk after a title indicates that the book is available in paperback.

1. Aldiss, Brian, *The Primal Urge.** A British farce about the conflict over the government's order that everyone must wear an ER (emotional response) disc attached to his forehead. The disc glows when the wearer is sexually stimulated. Lots of talk, little action, and practically no plot.

2. Anderson, Poul, *After Doomsday.** Earth has been destroyed, and only two space ships, one full of men, the other of women, survive. The sur-

[1]Three awards are of importance in science fiction: (1) the Hugo, given annually since 1953 by the World Science Fiction Convention; (2) the Nebula, given annually since 1965 by the Science Fiction Writers of America; (3) the International Fantasy Award, given annually from 1951 to 1957 by a panel of recognized experts.

vival of each group is unknown to the other and both set out to find beings like themselves so that the species can survive. They also look for the murderers of Earth. The plot is liberally sprinkled with clues for the reader. A good book that is too short.

3. Anderson, Poul, *Brain Wave.** All sentient beings on Earth undergo great increases in intelligence. Animals become as smart as human morons formerly were, morons as smart as ordinary humans, and ordinary humans become geniuses, causing upheaval and destruction of the social order.

4. Anderson, Poul, *The Enemy Stars.** Mankind is in the process of exploring the galaxy. It has sent out ships from which crews can return by matter transmitter. One crew suffers an emergency breakdown, and the story centers on the technical problems and personal relations between crew members. (This book was nominated for a Hugo in 1959).

5. Anderson, Poul, *The High Crusade.** Aliens land on Earth during the Middle Ages and are overcome by English soldiers preparing to embark on an invasion of France (the aliens have lost the art of hand-to-hand combat). The soldiers, their leader, and their whole village all board the spaceship to take it to France. Instead they wind up on one of the planets from which the aliens came. (Hugo nominee for 1961).

6. Anderson, Poul, *The Star Fox.** Gunnar Helm acts as a privateer in the service of the World Federation. The book is divided into three sections, and in all of them Helm is seeking to prevent the Aleriona from pushing the Federation forces back from the frontier worlds they hold. Lots of action. (One part, "Marque and Reprisal," was nominated for a 1966 Hugo and a 1965 Nebula.)

7. Anderson, Poul, *Tau Zero*.* A space ship's velocity approaches the speed of light, enabling it to cross from the Milky Way Galaxy to the Andromeda Galaxy in a few weeks (internal time). The ship is beset with mechanical problems, and its crew of fifty is beset with human problems. Both kinds are expertly handled by the author. (Hugo nominee 1971.)

8. Anderson, Poul and Dickson, Gordon, *Earthman's Burden*.* This book consists of a series of humorous stories about little teddy-bear-like creatures who have a passion for imitating certain characters and eras from Earth's history and literature.

9. Anthony, Piers, *Chthon*. Intricately constructed plot which interweaves past, present, and future so that the reader can discover the parallels in three subplots. The three foci of action all relate to the life of an individual in his boyhood, through his adult life, and into the time he spends as a criminal on a prison planet.

10. Anthony, Piers, *Macroscope*.* A giant crystal on a space station receives messages from 15,000 light years away. The information which is unraveled from the messages drives men insane. The crew of the space station is forced to flee with the crystal which provides them with answers to scientific problems and aids their escape. Finally, they find a massive complex which draws them into a world of symbology. (Hugo nominee 1970.)

11. Asimov, Isaac, *The Caves of Steel*.* A first rate science fiction mystery, using many of the basic Asimovian ideas about robots developed in his other stories. Investigators Lije Bailey (human) and R. Daneel (robot) combine their talents to solve a murder. Bailey's dislike for robots is gradually turned to respect by Daneel's quiet competence. (Sequel: *The Naked Sun*.)

12. Asimov, Isaac, *The Currents of Space.** In this story of political intrigue in a galactic civilization, "Crazy Rik" knows that Florina's sun is in its prenova stage and is psycho-probed to prevent the knowledge from leaking out. A Townman uses this information, with the help of the Trantorian Empire, to win the Florinians' freedom from the Sarkites.

13. Asimov, Isaac, *The Foundation Trilogy,* including *Foundation,** *Foundation and Empire,** and *Second Foundation.** The Foundations stand between the dissolution of the Galactic Empire and a "dark ages" of 30,000 years. Through the science of psychohistory, the Foundations can predict and ameliorate certain events, and this management of history reduces the interregnum to 1,000 years. The plot emphasizes the vast social forces in the Empire. (This trilogy won a Hugo in 1966 for the category of best all-time series.)

14. Asimov, Isaac, *Pebble in the Sky.** A nuclear lab accident knocks a man into an authoritarian future galactic society where, although mankind has spread to the stars, Earthmen are outcasts. Much of Earth itself is radioactive and euthanasia is practiced to keep the population from overcrowding the land that is left. An archeologist from "outside" comes to prove that the despised "earthies" are really the remnants of the original ancestors of the entire species.

15. Asimov, Isaac, *The Stars Like Dust.** The princeling of a planet attempts to overthrow a Galactic dictatorship. The plot involves a search for the Rebellion World, where weapons are being produced for the coming Revolution.

16. Bester, Alfred, *The Demolished Man.** A tycoon murders a competitor and detective Lincoln Powell has to establish a case against him. Powell, a telepath, uses his own and others'

psychic powers to pursue the case. Powell has to find the murdered man's daughter before the killer does (she witnessed the murder) and then has to force the murderer to confess because circumstances make it impossible to try him in court. The future society of this story is well developed and the zigzag plot is nicely executed. (Hugo winner 1953, International Fantasy Award nominee 1954.)

17. Bester, Alfred, *The Stars My Destination.** Gully Foyle is the sole survivor of a spacewreck. A passing ship ignores his pleas for help, but he is able to rescue himself, and then seeks revenge on those who ignored him. Psionic powers, teleportation, and Foyle's own obsessed personality play major parts in the plot.

18. Blish, James, *A Case of Conscience.** A Jesuit biologist is sent to study a planet peopled by reptiles as intelligent as man. Slowly, Father Sanchez comes to the realization that this alien life form presents humanity with a grave and unusual threat. (This book won the Hugo for 1959. The author considers it part of a philosophical trilogy which includes *Black Easter* and *Dr. Mirablis*.)

19. Blish, James, *The Cities in Flight Tetralogy,** including *Earthman, Come Home, They Shall Have Stars, The Triumph of Time, A Life for the Stars*. Flying Earth cities, called Okies, are powered by spindizzy fields. They travel throughout the galaxy selling whatever specialized services they have to offer. The series of stories covers a sweep of events and settings too detailed to recount here.

20. Blish, James, *Jack of Eagles.** A man discovers he has powers of unconscious precognition and sets out to discover his other talents. These discoveries lead him into trouble. First he loses his job, then he is alternately captured by the FBI, racketeers, and a secret organization of

other psychics who are planning to take over the world. With the aid of a friend and a scientist who is expert in parapsychology, he works to defeat the evil psychics.

21. Blish, James, *Titan's Daughter.** Giants (tetraploids) are created by genetic manipulation and are persecuted by the normal humans. The scientist-creator of the abnormally large humans is murdered and the hero is framed for it. Well-paced and interesting story.

22. Blish, James, *VOR.** A Michigan Civil Air Patrol unit discovers the wreckage of a space ship. They also discover that a creature has left the ship and is proceeding across the countryside destroying everything in its path. All efforts to stop it fail until a scientist and one of the CAP pilots discover the creature's inner weakness.

23. Bowen, John, *After the Rain.** A crackpot scientist's scheme to make water turns out to be disastrously successful—he causes a Second Flood. The plot concerns nine people who survive together on a balsa raft. The story emphasis is on the interactions of the crew. (This story was produced as a play on Broadway.)

24. Brackett, Leigh, *The Long Tomorrow.** The world has suffered an atomic war and, as a result, civilization has regressed to an agrarian level. Moreover, cities are viewed as having caused the war, and the new society has proscribed all things related to them. Young Len Coulter and his cousin Esau discover clues to a fabled city where that which has been forbidden still exists.

25. Bradbury, Ray, *Fahrenheit 451.** Books have been banned, and firemen, instead of putting out fires, set them whenever they find unburned books. Fireman Montag discovers that books aren't the threats to the social order he was told they were. This discovery leads to his downfall and flight.

59

26. Bradbury, Ray, *The Martian Chronicles.** This book is not really a novel, but a collection of related stories. A series of expeditions from Earth to Mars discloses a different reality to each group of explorers. Mars serves as a reflection of their differing expectations. The book has considerable charm, but some students may be puzzled by it.

27. Bradley, Marion Zimmer, *Sword of Aldones.* Lew Alton, a telepath, responds to an urgent call to return from exile to his home planet of Darkover. A half-breed Terran/Darkoverian, Alton is destined to play the central part in a telepathic power struggle between the Darkoverians who want more Terran control of their planet and those who want less. (Hugo nominee 1963.)

28. Brown, Frederic, *The Lights in the Sky Are Stars.** Max Andrews, a spaceman to the core, fights to keep Earth moving out to the solar system and beyond. He pursues his goal with great singlemindedness through political and physical adversities.

29. Brown, Frederic, *What Mad Universe.* A science fiction magazine editor is blasted into a parallel universe where he finds that, although many things are the same as in his own world, some important differences exist. For example, teleportation was discovered before the airplane, and what was science fiction in his former world is reality in his new world.

30. Brown, Rosel George, *Galactic Sibyl Sue Blue.** Sibyl Sue Blue is a policewoman circa 1990. Some humanoids from Centaurus have added her to their list of people to bump off. Eventually, she is kidnapped and discovers a plot to take over all the inhabited worlds. Although the heroine is the married mother of a teen-age daughter, she still comes across as a dynamic and sexually attractive individual.

31. Brunner, John, *Jagged Orbit*.* Super-gang industrial interests plan to reveal information about a new weapon in such a way that the black enclaves in society will be destroyed. In this world, antagonisms separate everyone. People live in heavily armed apartments and go out masked and armed. There is no interpersonal or intergroup trust. The story is an extrapolation of the result of a breakdown in the social contract and the development of the power of special interests. (1969 Nebula nominee.)

32. Brunner, John, *Stand on Zanzibar*.* The emphasis on style in this example of a "new wave" non-novel permits extremes in format (interspersed TV programs, unrelated bits of philosophy) and language (words are invented, shortened, combined, and made up of acronyms). The patchwork of disconnected episodes provides a montage of conditions in the world: overcrowding; personal relationships without meaning. Social psychologist and social dropout Chad Mulligan comments on the whole mess from a position of extreme disillusion. (Nebula nominee 1968, Hugo winner 1969.)

33. Budrys, Algis, *Rogue Moon*.* Men are sent to the moon by matter transmitter to explore a mysterious formation which kills them. The transmitter creates duplicates of the men, which are sacrificed to explore the formation. Each sacrifice adds a little more knowledge about the structure. Al Barker is the only man strong-minded enough to withstand the psychological trauma that comes when his alter ego is killed, and so he is used again and again. (Hugo nominee 1961.)

34. Budrys, Algis, *Who?*.* A top Western scientist is kidnapped by the Russians, mutilated in an explosion, and "rebuilt" with artificial body parts to the point where he is unrecognizable.

Finally, the Reds send him back. The dilemma: Is the person who is sent back who he says he is? Can he be trusted to go back to work on top-secret American projects? (Hugo nominee 1959.)

35. Christopher, John, *No Blade of Grass.** A virus destroys all the world's grasses, and consequently, a large part of the food supply. A man moves his family out of London (which is A-bombed) into the country where the chances of survival are greater. As they trek north, the situation forces them to become less and less civilized and more savage in order to survive.

36. Christopher, John, *Pendulum.** Teen-age motorcycle gangs take over British society. Action centers on the experiences of one middle class family during the revolt. The gangs are overthrown in the end, but the fabric of society is too torn to mend.

37. Clarke, Arthur C., *Childhood's End.** The Overlords' space ships appear over Earth, and enforce peace in the world. Attempts to discover their purpose fail, until they finally show themselves and the reason for their presence is revealed. A fine book.

38. Clarke, Arthur C., *The City and the Stars.** An expanded version of the earlier *Against the Fall of Night.* The time is Earth's far distant future, in the self-perpetuating city of Diaspar, which is surrounded by remnants of a great space empire. The main character is Alvin, a boy who wants to return to the days of the glorious past.

39. Clarke, Arthur C., *The Deep Range.** An undersea game warden rides herd on a group of whales, and tries to forget that he washed out of the space service. The story is packed with action and Clarke develops a number of ideas about man's possible future need to farm the sea.

40. Clarke, Arthur C., *Earthlight.** War between Earth and the Federation (comprised of Mars, Venus, and some of the solar system's larger satellites) seems imminent. Earth's colonies on the moon threaten to revolt and join the other side. Tensions are relaxed when Earthmen make a daring rescue of a disabled Federation ship. Well developed characterization and a detective story maintain the plot interest.

41. Clarke, Arthur C., *A Fall of Moondust.** A sightseeing sled on the moon is trapped 50 feet below the surface of a sea of dust when a sublunarean bubble bursts. The sled's captain is faced with the typical problems of panicky passengers, etc. Clarke does a superb job of taking this standard plot and putting in all the detailed extrapolations of scientific knowledge of the moon. A tense, realistic, and exciting drama. (Hugo nominee 1963.)

42. Clement, Hal, *Cycle of Fire.** The planet of Abyormen has two suns, which cause extreme changes in climate over a period of time. As a result, two widely divergent species develop, one that can live in extreme heat, the other in extreme cold. Each species dies out as its climate wanes. The plot is an account of the journey of a human space cadet and one of the "cool phase" natives, the arrival of another ship from Earth, and the decision the Earthmen must make about the future of the planet.

43. Clement, Hal, *Iceworld.** Earth is the iceworld, at least in the opinion of the natives of a planet (Sarr) with a sulphur vapor atmosphere. Someone is smuggling a drug (tobacco) to Sarr from Earth, and Sallman Ken, a Sarrian, sets out to uncover the dope runners.

44. Clement, Hal, *Mission of Gravity.** The planet of Mesklin is shaped like a disk instead of a

sphere, with a high rotation speed, high pressure hydrogen atmosphere, and other extremely non-Earth-like conditions. An Earth expedition makes contact with a Mesklinite representative and together they explore unfamiliar parts of the planet. This is the best example of Clement's stock-in-trade: ingenious and scientifically logical life forms and situations. (International Fantasy Award nominee 1953.)

45. Clement, Hal, *Needle*.* Alien detective chases alien criminal. They both crash in the Pacific, and each "takes over" the body of a human. The detective's problem, of course, is to find the human who has been possessed—like looking for a needle in a haystack.

46. Clement, Hal, *Starlight*.* Dhrawn, a kind of combination star-planet, is too massive to permit exploration by humans. So, they enlist the aid of Mesklinites (cf. *Mission of Gravity*) who can function in a high gravity environment. The Mesklinite leader's efforts to establish an unauthorized colony and the human leader's general distrust of non-humans lead to problems which endanger the explorers and their mission. (Hugo nominee 1970.)

47. Clifton, Mark and Riley, Frank, *They'd Rather Be Right*. A computer turns an old woman into a young and immortal beauty. The problem of immortality which is developed in this story is that people have to choose between keeping the beliefs they have always held and giving up their prejudices so that they can be malleable enough to live forever. (Hugo winner 1955.)

48. Compton, D.G., *The Steel Crocodile*.* Specialists in various scientific fields work at an institute where a computer analyzes and synthesizes world wide research and makes reports on it. Behind the scenes, the institute manages the

news of some discoveries and attempts to direct society in certain ways. A special secret project, complete with murder mystery, enlivens the story. (Nebula nominee 1970.)

49. Compton, D.G., *Synthajoy.** A machine which records inner sensations has become popular and the inventor is working on another machine which will reproduce all known sensations. The inventor's wife has moral objections to the idea of counterfeiting experiences. When her husband is murdered, she is put in a mental institution. Most of the story is concerned with why she went mad and the process by which she returns to reality. The book contains more depth of characterization than the typical Sf book.

50. Cooper, Edmund, *Seed of Light.** The few survivors of an atomic war live in domed cities. They send out a spaceship, but it discovers no other habitable planets in its 1,000—year journey. Finally, the explorers decide to try their subspace drive. Somehow it returns them to Earth 50,000 years before the development of civilized man, where they set up a colony which is eventually discovered by early man.

51. De Camp, L. Sprague, *Divide and Rule.* "Hoppers" invade Earth and set up a feudal society with ultra modern knights and all the conveniences which might have resulted if King Arthur had had the services of a modern industrial engineer. The future society apes the feudal society of Earth's past.

52. De Camp, L. Sprague, *Lest Darkness Fall.* A stroke of lightning takes Martin Padway back in time to 6th Century Rome. In his efforts to adjust to his new environment, he introduces a number of "inventions" which earn him the reputation of being a wizard. He also gets involved in politics. With his "inventions" and his knowledge of history, he tries to alter

events so that the Dark Ages will not come.

53. De Camp, L. Sprague, *Rogue Queen.** One of De Camp's "Viagens" stories. On Ormazd, the Avtines (humanoids) have developed a social structure which resembles that of Earth's bees (queens, neuter females, workers, warriors, and drones). Iroedh, a queen, tries to overthrow the social order with the aid of an Earth expedition.

54. De Camp, L. Sprague and Miller, P. Schuyler, *Genus Homo.** A bus load of travelers is caught in a landslide and emerges one million years in the future. The world is controlled by intelligent Earth animals who live in an organized society. They treat the people like zoo specimens. Reader interest must depend on the human-animal reversal since there is no plot and little characterization. At the end of a gorilla-baboon war, the book just stops.

55. Delany, Samuel, *Babel-17.** Poetess and language expert Rydra Wong is engaged by General Forester of the Alliance to decipher an unknown language called Babel-17 which is used by the Invaders in their attacks on Alliance installations. Her investigation involves her in intrigue and her life is threatened by the sabotage of her space ship. (Hugo nominee 1967, Nebula winner 1966 (in a tie).

56. Delany, Samuel, *The Einstein Intersection.* Aliens enter the bodies of humans in order to revitalize mankind which has become stagnant. This book is a good example of the difference between the new Sf writers of the late sixties and early seventies and the older writers who were popular in the period of the forties and fifties. (Nebula winner 1967, Hugo nominee 1968.)

57. Delany, Samuel, *Nova.** This story is too difficult to describe in much detail because of the wealth of action, color, and imaginative and

improbable combinations of concepts from myths, mysticism, philosophy, politics, and sociology. Three readers could read this story from three entirely different perspectives. (Hugo nominee 1969.)

58. Del Rey, Lester, *Nerves.** An accident occurs in an atomic power plant. The problems of political pressures and the frantic efforts to keep the accident from becoming a real catastrophe make for a tense and realistic plot. The main character is Dr. Ferrel, the medical officer, who must deal with the physical and mental traumas suffered by the plant workers.

59. Dick, Philip K., *Do Androids Dream of Electric Sheep?** Dick writes stories with strange and wondrous plots, and this one is no exception. Earthmen feel threatened by the large and growing number of androids that may replace them. Rick Decard is a bounty hunter looking for six androids who have escaped from Mars to Earth. And from then on, things really get complicated. (1968 Nebula nominee.)

60. Dick, Philip K., *Eye in the Sky.** A Bevatron particle accelerator goes wrong somewhere, and an assortment of people find themselves in a strange and illogical world. Eventually they discover that the "world" they're in is in the unconscious mind of one of the members of their own group.

61. Dick, Philip K., *The Man in the High Castle.** The setting for this story is the U.S.—a U.S. which has been split up between the Japanese and Germans following their victory in WWII in 1947. The story opens fifteen years after the end of the war. It concerns conflicts of interest and espionage between the two ruling powers and the resistance of some of the conquered Americans. (1963 Hugo winner.)

62. Dickson, Gordon, *The Genetic General.** A planet's chief export is skilled mercenaries. Donal

Graeme is one of these young soldiers (bred and trained to fight) who eventually rises to a high position in the military branch of galactic society. (Hugo nominee 1960, runner-up to the winner. Many of Dickson's stories fit into the same projected future. This is one of them.)

63. Dickson, Gordon, *Naked to the Stars.** A soldier of the future discovers that he is too much of a non-conformist to remain in the army. Following a memory lapse during combat he leaves the military and joins the Contacts Service which attempts to understand alien cultures. Soldiers are scornful of Contacts agents because they view them as weaklings who are afraid to fight. The book contains weighty questions on the rightness of war.

64. Dickson, Gordon, *Necromancer (No Room For Man).** Engineer Paul Formain lost an arm in an accident, and the remaining one develops unusual powers. Then he learns of an organization which claims it can grow him another. The intricate plot involves magic (Alternate Laws) and an attempt to overthrow Earth's technological civilization. (Fits Dickson's projected future.)

65. Dickson, Gordon, *Soldier Ask Not.** A man sets out to avenge the death of his brother-in-law at the hands of the "friendlies." (Part of this book, under the same title, won a short fiction Hugo award in 1965. This book fits into the projected history.)

66. Farmer, Philip Jose, *Flesh.** A returned space ship discovers that Earth's civilization has been reduced to a few isolated pastoral societies. One of these, Deecee, selects the ship's captain to be the main male character in a six month's long fertility rite. During this time, several other communities with equally strange sexual mores also come on the scene.

67. Farmer, Philip Jose, *The Green Odyssey.** Alan Green, space-wrecked on a feudal planet, hears of an Earth ship which landed a few thousand miles away. He sets out to reach it so that he can go home. The journey to the ship is his odyssey.

68. Farmer, Philip Jose, *The Lovers.* A future society exhibits such strong puritanical traits that, for example, a normal marriage relationship in contemporary America would be considered obscene and perverted. Much of this possible future is extrapolated from some features of our own world and should be viewed in that light. Eventually the inhibited hero comes into contact with a woman from a less restrictive culture who succeeds in shaking his beliefs.

69. Frank, Pat, *Alas, Babylon.** Thirty-two-year-old lawyer Randy Bragg lives in Florida in an old Victorian home that has been in his family for three generations. His brother, an Air Force Intelligence officer, warns him that a Russian nuclear attack is likely and sends his family to live with Randy. The rest of the story concerns Randy's partly inept, partly skillful, attempt to deal with atomic catastrophe and the subsequent breakdown in civilization that follows. A well paced and generally believable story.

70. Galouye, Daniel, *Dark Universe.** Jared Fenton has grown up in a cavern world of Darkness where his people have developed hearing and smell as their principal senses. His life is threatened by radiation-mutated giant bats and Zivvers, humans who "see" by sensing heat (infrared radiation). Then comes a new threat—vile smelling Monsters and their screaming silent sound. (Hugo nominee 1962.)

71. Garrett, Randall, *Too Many Magicians.** The Plan-

69

tagenet kings rule England, France, and America and an East/West conflict exists between Poland and England. The laws of magic stand in place of the laws of science of our world. Espionage compounded by mysterious murders at a magicians' convention form the basic interest and direction for the plot. (Hugo nominee 1967.)

72. Gordon, Rex, *First on Mars*. After crashlanding on Mars, an engineer lives a Robinson Crusoe-like existence for fifteen years. The realistic documentary style gives an interesting picture of the problem of survival in an alien and hostile world.

73. Gordon, Rex, *First to the Stars*. Astronauts discover at blast-off that there is an error in the direction of their spaceship. They land on a distant planet, the spaceship sinks into the mud, and the female astronaut eventually dies in childbirth. The survivors are taken to live on an alien planet where they must adjust to the alien culture. The author muffed a good chance to develop the problems involved when a human child is raised among non-humans.

74. Harness, Charles, *The Rose*.* The theme of this story concerns the relationship between science and art. The characters, a psychiatrist and her patient (an artist), and his wife (a scientist), are merely vehicles for the author's ideas. The story ends on a fantastic note: the main female character sprouts wings and dies while she is performing a ballet in which she transmutes some scientific equations into music. Very philosophical and avant-garde.

75. Harrison, Harry, *Deathworld*.* Adventurer Jason din Alt arrives on Pyrrus and finds a fantastic struggle going on between the human colonists and the entire range of native flora and fauna. Jason's problem is three-fold: to preserve his own life, to measure up to the colo-

nists' rigorous view of manhood, and to find out why the planet's ecology, which was originally benign, has become so lethal. (Hugo nominee 1961. Sequels: *Deathworld 2, Deathworld 3*.)

76. Harrison, Harry, *Planet of the Damned.* The planet of Dis is threatening to wipe out its neighbor Nyjord. Troubleshooter Brion Brandd is sent in to solve the problem before Nyjord acts in self-defense and smashes Dis first. Lots of violence and blood-and-guts type action. (Hugo nominee 1962.)

77. Harrison, Harry, *The Stainless Steel Rat.** Slippery Jim De Griz is one of the best con men in the Galaxy. But he's finally trapped by the police and forced to help them catch an even bigger criminal. A swashbuckling adventure detective story. Good fun. (Sequel: *The Stainless Steel Rat's Revenge*)

78. Heinlein, Robert, *Beyond This Horizon.** In this society, men carry sidearms and settle differences of opinion *a la* the Old West, and geneticists try to tailor human strains. Hamilton Felix is the product of such tailoring, but resists playing his part in continuing the development of his particular strain (by marrying a woman whom the scientists recommend). However, he eventually changes his mind. This early Heinlein book is one of his best.

79. Heinlein, Robert, *The Door into Summer.** An inventor is cheated out of his business by his girlfriend and his partner (who are lovers). He goes into suspended animation to escape this traumatic situation, is revived 30 years later, and has some trouble fitting into the technologically advanced society. Eventually he finds a scientist with a time machine and goes back to do some legal maneuvering which ruins his partner's scheme. He then goes into cold sleep again. Very enjoyable story.

80. Heinlein, Robert, *Double Star.** Actor Lorenzo Smythe is talked into impersonating an important public figure, one who has been kidnapped, so that his part in an important ceremony will be filled and his enemies will not be able to gain from the disappearance. The impersonation is carried out in a number of strange places over an increasingly long period of time. (Hugo winner 1956.)

81. Heinlein, Robert, *Have Space Suit—Will Travel.** A teen-age boy wins a secondhand spacesuit in a soap slogan contest, refurbishes it, and then is off on a series of adventures on the Moon, Pluto, a planet of Vega, and the Lesser Magellanic Cloud. That progression of events may sound a little fantastic, but you won't think so when you read the book. (Hugo nominee 1959.)

82. Heinlein, Robert, *The Moon Is a Harsh Mistress.** The Moon has been turned into a penal colony and it takes tough characters to survive in the harsh conditions. The prisoners have formed a society which reflects the peculiar living conditions of their prison. Since the colony is exploited by Earth, it plans and prosecutes a revolution to free itself. Much of the book is concerned with the mechanics of political science and revolution. (Hugo nominee 1966, Nebula nominee 1966, Hugo winner 1967.)

83. Heinlein, Robert, *Orphans of the Sky.** A huge spaceship is sent out to colonize another star system. It runs afoul of a mutiny. Gradually the inhabitants and their descendants forget not only their mission, but also that they are on a spaceship. Through the years the inhabitants create a mythology that explains their situation. Young Hugh Hoyland becomes curious about his world and eventually establishes an alliance with the outlaw mutants.

Together they bring the ship to a safe landing.

84. Heinlein, Robert, *Podkayne of Mars.** Mars-born Podkayne Fries and her (she thinks) evil genius brother Clarke con their uncle and a number of other people into letting them accompany him on a trip to Venus. Once there, they become involved in some interplanetary intrigue which results in their being kidnapped to prevent their uncle from attending an important political conference.

85. Heinlein, Robert, *The Puppet Masters.** A chilling tale of aliens from Titan (one of Jupiter's moons) who parasitically attach themselves to men's backs and control them. Fast moving story about the U.S. government intelligence agents who attempt to discover the weaknesses of the invaders so that they can be defeated. You won't be able to stop reading.

86. Heinlein, Robert, *Sixth Column (The Day After Tomorrow).** The U.S. Army is all but destroyed by the PanAsian invaders. A small group of men in the Citadel, a secret underground installation, survive and finish developing a secret weapon which utilizes the Ledbetter Effect. Six of the men set up an underground counter-invasion organization using the establishment of a new religion as a cover.

87. Heinlein, Robert, *Starship Troopers.** In a future society based on militarism, veterans are given preference for governmental positions, courses in militaristic patriotism are required in school, and people can't become full-fledged citizens unless they serve in the army. The focus of the story is the life of a Mobile Infantryman from enlistment through his rise to the position of a seasoned officer. The book is the author's vehicle for conveying his own opinions about the proper place of the military in society. (Hugo winner 1960.)

88. Heinlein, Robert, *Stranger in a Strange Land.** This

book is too long and complex to really explain here. The main character, Valentine Michael Smith, is raised by Martians and returns to the fold of humanity only as an adult. Because of his alien upbringing, he has acquired a number of attitudes and skills which make him very different from ordinary humans. Heinlein uses this story to attack a number of aspects of society. He also suggests some new directions in the areas of love and sex and personal freedom. (Hugo winner 1962.)

89. Heinlein, Robert, *Waldo*. A genius suffering from myasthenia gravis (extremely weak muscles) lives in a space platform and invents gadgets to make his life easier. The concept of parallel worlds plays a part in the plot. (One of Waldo's inventions is a set of mechanical hands which artificially multiply what little strength he does have. Some atomic lab workers must have read this story, because the mechanical-electrical "hands" which they use to handle radioactive materials have been nicknamed "waldoes.")

90. Henderson, Zenna, *Pilgrimage—The Book of the People.** Long ago, a space ship containing The People (who have ESP powers) crashed on Earth. Some of the survivors develop and maintain a colony which continues to exist into modern times. The members of the colony continue to have knowledge of themselves which enables them to protect and maintain their separate existence. Descendants of other survivors are scattered around the world and are gradually recognized and brought to the colony. Reader identification comes from feelings many people have about being "different." A substantial book. (Sequel: *The People: No Different Flesh**)

91. Herbert, Frank, *Dune.** This long book contains a number of interweaving plot lines which make

it difficult to describe in capsule form. Herbert has created a whole world *cum* desert ecology *cum* society in considerable detail. The color, action, and conceptual innovations of the story are definitely worth the reader's time. (Hugo nominee 1964, Hugo winner 1966 for an enlarged version, Nebula winner 1965. Sequel: *Dune Messiah.**)

92. Herbert, Frank, *Dragon in the Sea* (*21st Century Sub*).* The East and West engage in undersea submarine skirmishes. One such sub, the *Fenian Ram,* serves as the setting for the physical dangers of undersea warfare, a spy hunt, sabotage, and the extreme psychological tensions and pressures in which men work.

93. Howard, Hayden, *The Eskimo Invasion.** Some Eskimos have been placed on a reservation where they are forced to re-learn their ancestors' ways of arctic survival. Somehow, the Eskimo breeding rate increases tremendously. A population expert is sent to study them and concludes that they represent a new species of human. The expert, Dr. Joe West, is confronted with a number of problems when he tries to act on behalf of the Eskimo, not the least of which is what to do with his constantly pregnant Eskimo wife. (Hugo nominee—short version—1967, Nebula nominee 1966, Nebula nominee 1967.)

94. Hoyle, Fred, *The Black Cloud.** An astronomical cloud threatens to blot out the sun. The plot centers on the world's adjustment to the news and its preparation for the catastrophe. Surprise twist near the end.

95. Hoyle, Fred and Eliot, John, *A for Andromeda.** Contact with ET's (extra-terrestrial aliens) is established by radio over a distance of 200 light years. The aliens send radio instructions to build a computer which eventually learns enough human technology so that it can di-

rect men to build an android representative of the alien race. The trick is that the android (and the computer) have been designed to conquer the Earth.

96. Jones, D.F., *Implosion*. This book is an account of population problems in reverse. Many English women and animals have become sterile. A government program to care for the fertile ones and to induce greater childbearing leads to failure when it is discovered that the grandchildren are invariably boys. The main character is John Bart, physician and politician. The plot concerns his personal problems when his young wife is taken off to the baby farm and he subsequently takes up with her twin sister.

97. Judd, Cyril (pen name of Cyril Kornbluth and Judith Merril in collaboration), *Gunner Cade*.* Gunner Cade is a skillful, dedicated, but naive member of the ascetic Order of Armsmen and as such is pledged to defend the Emperor. Although space travel exists between Earth and Mars, the society has reverted to a feudalistic state. The plot centers on a young armsman who is disabused of his beliefs in his world, and his involvement in the struggle of the Marsmen for their independence from Earth.

98. Keyes, Daniel, *Flowers for Algernon*.* The story of the struggle of a 32-year-old retarded man to achieve emotional maturity after an experimental operation provides him with a rapidly accelerating intelligence. He has problems in trying to fit into society as a genius, just as he had other problems in trying to fit in as a moron. Gradually his intelligence subsides and he becomes a dullard again. Smart or dumb, Charly has great charisma. (Hugo winner 1960—short version; Hugo nominee 1967, Nebula winner 1966. Also formed

basis for a play and a movie which were nominated for Hugos in 1962 and 1969 respectively.)

99. Knight, Damon, *Hell's Pavement* (*The Analogue Men*).* In this future society, people have been forcefully provided with "angels", psychological constructs which compel them to do, or not to do, certain things. Young Arthur Bass has no angel—he's one of the few people who are naturally resistant to the process —and this deviation causes him to leave his position in society and join an underground of others like himself.

100. Kornbluth, C.M., *Not This August.* The U.S. loses WW II to the Russians and Chinese, who divide up the country and set up occupation forces. The story presents a believable picture of how easily many Americans could adapt to foreign occupation forces (as other countries have). The underground which inevitably forms finds it tough going until they discover they have an ace-in-the-hole.

101. Kornbluth, C.M., *Syndic.* A post WW III world is structured along the lines of organized crime syndicates. The Syndic runs the east, the Mob the west, and the third force is the Government, based in Ireland. A Syndic man goes underground to spy on the Government and winds up with a different outlook on his world.

102. Kornbluth, C. M. and Pohl, Frederik, *Gladiator-at-Law.* * This extrapolation of a future society includes a giant corporation which controls the housing industry around which the social structure revolves. People without corporate contacts live in ghettoes and provide the Field Day crowds with scenes of carnage. Lawyer Charles Mundin takes on the power structure.

103. Kornbluth, C. M. and Pohl, Frederik, *The Space Merchants.* * This future society features the

problems of too many people and too few resources, all of it run to the tune of Madison
Avenue style huckstering and exploitation.
Minor executive Mitchell Courtenay loses his
status in an ad firm and fights his way back
to power with the aid of an underground organization.

104. Kornbluth, C. M. and Pohl, Frederik, *Wolfbane.**
Earth has been kidnapped by another world.
The two orbit around the Moon, which has
been turned into an artificial sun. Blue pyra-
mids control the world, and rebels, called
"wolves", set out to save the world from the
alien masters.

105. Kuttner, Henry, *Fury (Destination Infinity)*.* Sam
Reed, an outcast from the Immortal aristoc-
racy which rules an undersea kingdom,
launches a revolt against the rulers. He discovers that he is also an Immortal when his
first coup fails. Eventually he forces mankind
from the security of undersea life. He launches
them on a new drive to tame the land masses
of their planet (Venus) and from there on-
ward into space.

106. Kuttner, Henry, *Mutant.** This series of related
stories is about the Baldies, hairless mutant
telepaths born after an atomic war. The Baldies are feared by ordinary humans, are hunted
like animals, and are consequently concerned
with self-preservation. Two factions are in
conflict: a paranoid group that wants to wipe
out ordinary humans, and moderates who are
trying to find a way to give ordinary humans
telepathic power.

107. Kuttner, Henry, *The Time Axis.* Jeremy Cortland
has a near brush with death from nekron (neg-
ative matter). With three others, he goes to the
time axis and then into the far future to remove
the nekron from history. When this battle is
won, the four finally see the Face of Ea in

which Jeremy recognizes the features of a super robot he had seen being constructed in the future. This eschatological vision suggests a final amalgam of man and his machines.

108. Lafferty, R. A., *Fourth Mansions.* As with Lafferty's *Past Master* (see below), it is difficult to say exactly what this book is about. For one thing, seven people set out to reshape the world. But the characters and their concerns change so much from beginning to end that the reader is not exactly sure what is going on. (Nebula nominee 1970.)

109. Lafferty, R. A., *Past Master.* Sir Thomas More is plucked out of his own time just before his execution and thrown into the company of an odd lot of characters including a witch, a monk, a mutant sea animal, a necromancer, some Programmed People, and others. These characters become involved in a number of situations which illustrate the human condition (among other things). You may find more than one reading helpful in understanding this one. (Hugo nominee 1969, Nebula nominee 1968.)

110. Laumer, Keith, *Galactic Diplomat.* A series of stories about James Retief, an officer in Earth's diplomatic corps, and his efforts to help Earth establish her power in the face of opposition by various nonhuman groups who want to extend their own influence.

111. Laumer, Keith, *A Plague of Demons.* CBI agent John Bravais is sent to discover the reason for an unusual number of disappearances of soldiers in a UN-supervised war between Algeria and Morocco. He discovers that aliens are spiriting the soldiers away. He undergoes special surgical implants in his body which augment his physical capabilities so that he can investigate further. Fast moving story. (Nebula nominee 1965.)

112. Laumer, Keith, and Brown, Rosel George, *Earth-blood*. A human boy is raised by a humanoid couple in a ghetto on one of the worlds in a galactic empire. He is kidnapped twice, once into a circus, and a second time into a space pirate's ship. He eventually winds up in the Terran Navy. At the end of the book the secret of his ancestry is revealed. Lots of color and action. (Nebula nominee 1966.)

113. LeGuin, Ursula K., *The Left Hand of Darkness*.* The planet of Gethen, called "Winter" by the galactic government which sends an envoy to establish diplomatic relations, is in a perpetual ice age with huge glacial ice-caps covering most of both northern and southern hemispheres. The people of Gethen have a civilization about as advanced as Earth's Middle Ages (politically and socially). Also, each individual has the potential of becoming either male or female once a month. All these factors combine to provide an interesting plot and a fascinating development of the nature of love. (Nebula winner 1969, Hugo winner 1970.)

114. Leiber, Fritz, *The Big Time*.* The Change War over the structure of history is being waged between Spiders and Snakes. An assortment of combatants in the war take an R&R break in a place between times and worlds where personalities eventually clash. The whole place is threatened by an atomic bomb scare. (Hugo winner 1958.)

115. Leiber, Fritz, *Gather, Darkness*.* A religious theocracy maintains itself with the superstitious masses by causing "miracles" through the application of scientific discoveries. A secret opposition organization uses "witchcraft" (more science) to combat the dictatorship.

116. Leiber, Fritz, *The Green Millenium*.* It's this way. There's this green cat that enters the life of

Phil Gish. A number of strange people want it and are willing to commit all sorts of mayhem to get it. Colorful, complex tangle of plot and characters in a near-future setting.

117. Leiber, Fritz, *The Wanderer.** A maverick planet called the Wanderer rebels at cosmic justice and flees in and out of sub-space. The effects of its appearance near Earth are detailed in a series of episodes which cause world-wide disaster. The concept of rebellion against authority is played out against a counterpoint of resultant world-wide disorders. Not for beginning readers because of its diffuse structure. (Hugo winner 1965.)

118. Leinster, Murray, (pen name of William F. Jenkins), *The Pirates of Zan.* Bron Heddan, a scion of the pirates of the planet Zan, runs off to Walden to be an electronics engineer. One of his inventions gets him in trouble there, so he flees to Earth and winds up pirating some machinery to help out some hapless emigrants stranded there. (Hugo nominee 1960.)

119. MacDonald, John D., *The Girl, the Gold Watch and Everything.** Humorous plot about a man who obtains a gold watch which slows down time. He picks up a girlfriend (a nightclub singer) and has a number of adventures with her and some other girls.

120. Matheson, Richard, *I Am Legend.** An epidemic has caused all of mankind to turn into vampires. Robert Neville did not catch the disease. Every night he is besieged by vampires in his town who want his blood. The reasons for this situation, and his problems in struggling to survive, are the main concerns of the plot.

121. McCaffrey, Anne, *Dragonflight.** On the planet of Pern, intelligent dragon-like creatures and men combine in a kind of symbiotic relationship that begins at the dragon's birth. Every 200 years another planet approaches close

enough so that Threads can fall onto Pern. The dragons and their riders are all that stand between the Threads and the destruction of Pern. At the time of the story we see the human culture on Pern has all but forgotten the reason for the dragon riders' existence. (Short version Hugo nominee 1969. Nebula winner 1968.)

122. McCaffrey, Anne, *Restoree.** An old maid is kidnapped by creatures in a flying saucer. She is given a new body and a job as an attendant in a sort of psychiatric ward. From here she launches a revolution against her captors. Thorough development of the details of an alien feudal-type culture.

123. McCaffrey, Anne, *The Ship Who Sang.** In this story, spaceships have minds and personalities. One of them, Helva, is a little different because she can sing. Her adventures, her relationships with humans, and her special problems resulting from the fact that she has human emotions, but not a human body, form the trappings of the story.

124. McCann, Edison (pen name of Lester Del Rey and Frederik Pohl in collaboration), *Preferred Risk.** This extrapolation of a future society follows the pattern of *The Space Merchants.* In this case, insurance companies run the world. Tom Wills, a company man, becomes entangled in behind-the-scenes intrigue which shows him the company's base motives.

125. McIntosh, J. T. (pen name of James MacGregor), *The Fittest (The Rule of the Pagbeasts).** Biological experimentation with animals (increasing their intelligence) succeeds too well, and mankind is soon fighting these hybrids for survival. The story centers on the Paget family whose father created the animal geniuses and who are hunted by men and animals.

126. McIntosh, J. T., *One in Three Hundred.* Earth is

threatened with cosmic destruction and only one in three hundred can be saved. Story centers on selection of the lucky ones and on their transportation to Mars where they go about building a new world from the old.

127. Mead, Shepard, *The Big Ball of Wax.** A satire about the happy world of merchandising in the future. A female evangelist has appropriated a scientific discovery which can artificially produce sensations in the brain. She tries to use this to sell her brand of religion. Naturally she runs afoul of others interested in using the device themselves.

128. Merril, Judith, *The Tomorrow People.** Johnny Wendt, a space hero, has mental problems because of the mysterious loss of his partner during their exploration of Mars. Lisa Trove, his mistress, visits the Moon colony and discovers that she has ESP powers which she uses to help Johnny solve his partner's disappearance. Well developed characters face understandable psychological problems. Might be especially good for girls.

129. Miller, Walter M., Jr., *A Canticle for Leibowitz.** A new Dark Age has settled on the world following an atomic holocaust. The Catholic Church is the preserver of learning. The book is divided into three sections, 600 years apart, and follows the rise of a new technological civilization which the Church tries in vain to help avoid the mistakes of the past. (Hugo winner 1961.)

130. Moore, C. L., *Doomsday Morning.** The authoritarian government suspects a revolt is coming. A down-and-out actor is given a job—to travel the countryside with a stock company giving a certain performance at every stop. The purpose of the assignment? Read the book.

131. Moore, Ward, *Bring the Jubilee.* Suppose that Lee had defeated Grant at Gettysburg. The Indus-

trial Revolution in the North would have been halted; the South would have expanded into Latin America; the West would not have been so easily won. And so on.

132. Moore, Ward, and Davidson, Avram, *Joyleg.* * It is discovered that an old man in the Tennessee hills is drawing a veteran's pension—dating from the Revolutionary War! His secret elixir is (of course) a certain type of moonshine. This rather startling information causes him to become the center of a lot of attention from Congress and others. Humorous.

133. Niven, Larry, *Ringworld.* * Ringworld is a huge ring-shaped artificial world with a sun at its center. The four main characters are sent to explore it, crash-land there, and experience a series of adventures on their journey through this unusual and amazing world. The development of Ringworld's fascinating nature is the main story interest. (Nebula winner 1970, Hugo winner 1971).

134. Norton, Andre, *Beast Master.* * A Navaho Indian is one of the few survivors of a planet destroyed by aliens called Xik. The Indian has an empathic/telepathic relation with certain animals. With them as partners, he hires out to settlers on the planet of Arzor as a scout. His adventures lead him to encounters with outlaws, Xik, and an unknown race. (Sequel: *Lord of Thunder.* *)

135. Norton, Andre, *The Defiant Agents.* * East/West competition is carried into time travel when American Indian Time Agents are sent to colonize the planet of Topaz, where they discover Russian Tartars are already in residence. Good action adventure space opera. (Related stories: *The Time Traders,* * *Galactic Derelict,* * *Key Out of Time.* *)

136. Norton, Andre, *Star Rangers* (*The Last Planet*).* Patrol Ship Starfire crashes on a strange de-

serted planet. The survivors—Rangers, Patrol men (including humans and non-humans)— find a deserted city and another group of castaways. Soon they face new threats and discover the planet's secret.

137. Norton, Andre, *The X-Factor.** Misfit youngster Diskan Fentress steals a spaceship and runs away from home to land on an unsettled world. He meets some creatures called the Brothers-in-Fur who can communicate with him telepathically. They show him a ruined city where he finds survivors of a previous expedition.

138. Nourse, Alan, *Raiders from the Rings.* The personnel of the military outposts of various nations on the Moon and planets refuse to fight when WW III breaks out on Earth and are consequently exiled. They create a new society of Spacers and periodically raid Earth for women and booty. Three teenagers wade through several mysteries in their quest to end the Earth/Spacer feud.

139. Oliver, Chad, *Shadows in the Sun.** Anthropologist Paul Ellery discovers that a small town in Texas has been entirely taken over by aliens. Their purpose, he finds, is to "colonize" earth by slowly replacing humans in all small towns, thereby forcing Earthmen into city reservations. Ellery is given the chance to join the aliens.

140. Pangborn, Edgar, *Davy.** A Third World War has caused the oceans to rise, mutant births, and the world to regress to a level of civilization like that of the 1700's. The story centers on a young boy who grows to manhood *a la* Tom Jones. The author has neatly altered the upper New York State/New England countryside to create a very believable post-atomic war wilderness. (Hugo nominee 1965.)

141. Pangborn, Edgar, *A Mirror for Observers.** This "journal" details a Martian Observer's strug-

gle with a former colleague and with human social forces for supremacy in directing the development of Angelo Pontevecchio, a genius whose contribution to world affairs could hasten mankind's progress toward Union or self-destruction. The underlying theme of the conflict is Man's need for an ethical system based on love of one's fellow man. (International Fantasy Award winner, 1955.)

142. Pangborn, Edgar, *West of the Sun.* Earthmen in search of a habitable planet land on Lucifer, which already has two intelligent but primitive humanoid species. The humans try to build a new society with the natives, but fail, and move to an isolated island to rebuild.

143. Panshin, Alexei, *Rite of Passage.** This is the story of Mia Havero, who grows up on a starship that is a world unto itself. The nomadic existence sets the ship's inhabitants apart from the colonists on the worlds they visit. At the age of 14, children on the ship are set down on any of a number of uncivilized worlds to survive for a month and thus prove they are entitled to pass into adulthood. (Hugo nominee 1969, Nebula winner 1968.)

144. Phillips, Mark (pen name of Randall Garrett and Laurence Janifer in collaboration), *Brain Twister.* The FBI is trying to track down a telepathic spy and enlists the aid of another telepath—a little old lady who thinks she is Queen Elizabeth I. The book's comedic plot calls for one FBI agent to pretend to be Henry VIII in order to cope with "Her Majesty's" idiosyncracies. Even though she leads them to the spy, she gives the answers in such a way that the agent still has to rely on his own logic to puzzle out the solution. (Hugo nominee 1960. Sequels: *Supermind** and *The Impossibles.**)

145. Piper, H. Beam, *Little Fuzzy.** The Zarathustra

Company can completely control and exploit a planet if there is no intelligent life on it. Small fuzzy creatures are belatedly discovered after colonization begins. The company has a vested interest in seeing that the subsequent investigation shows that the creatures are not intelligent. A delightfully comic story. (Hugo nominee 1963. Sequel: *The Other Human Race.*)

146. Pohl, Frederik, *Drunkard's Walk.* This extrapolation of a future society centers on overpopulation and trends in education. The hero is a math instructor. Someone is trying to kill him by telepathically forcing him to commit suicide.

147. Pohl, Frederik, *Slave Ship.* Animals are trained to "man" a warship so they can replace men who are not expendable. Eventually, the Navy sends an animal ship into enemy territory on a secret mission.

148. Pratt, Fletcher, *The Undying Fire.* Captain Thorwald Paulsson is railroaded out of the Space Command. He sets out to discover the secret of a neptunium motor to redeem himself. Space opera.

149. Robinson, Frank, *The Power.* The Superman-ESP theme of this book is carried out in a murder mystery setting which sees one principal character after another being bumped off, and an innocent man on the run for the killings. (Provided basis for movie *The Power.*)

150. Russ, Joanna, *And Chaos Died.* A man is thrown into a utopian psi society on another planet. From living in it he gradually develops psi powers himself. Then he returns to Earth and is able to look at its society from the inside. The author is rather successful at giving the reader a look at what it feels like to be a telepath. (Nebula nominee 1970.)

151. Russell, Eric Frank, *Sinister Barrier.* Men are treated as pets by an invisible alien race. Bill

Graham must solve the mystery of the peril by finding out what 20 murdered scientists had discovered. Fast moving adventure.

152. Schmitz, James H., *The Universe Against Her.** Telepath Telzey Amberdon tackles the Establishment, in particular the bureaucracy of the psychology Service. One of the better Sf books with a female protagonist.

153. Schmitz, James H., *The Witches of Karres.** Spaceship Captain Pausert rescues a teenage witch from her nasty owner. He then further complicates his life by buying her two younger sisters. With these three free spirits on his hands his life becomes increasingly hectic, to the point where he becomes involved in espionage, piracy, and a secret galactic war. (Hugo nominee 1967.)

154. Shaw, Bob, *The Two Timers.** Standard time travel plot wherein a man goes back to prevent a tragedy from happening. The characterization makes this story a cut above the average.

155. Sheckley, Robert, *Immortality Inc.** A yacht designer is killed in a car accident in 1958, but scientists from the year 2110 save him by pulling him into the future and putting him in a new body. The company which brought him through time wants to use him as an advertising gimmick. But the plan falls through and he finds it necessary to go out into this strange new world to find a place for himself. (Hugo nominee 1959.)

156. Sheckley, Robert, *Journey Beyond Tomorrow.** Joenes, an innocent from the South Seas, tours the centers of civilization according to an account pieced together from old South Seas documents. In this parallel to the travels of Odysseus, a number of mythological names come up and some of the episodes are recognizable. There isn't enough character development in Joenes to balance the lack of plot.

157. Shiras, William, *Children of the Atom.* A group of stories about mutant children with vast mental superiority over normals. The children are discovered by Dr. Peter Welles who organizes a secret school for them so they can receive the special attention they need.

158. Silverberg, Robert, *The Masks of Time.* As the year 2000 approaches, a world-wide cult comes to believe that the world will end on that date. Vronan-19, ostensibly from the future, appears and is given a cook's tour of the world which provides the author with an opportunity to comment on world conditions. Although the book is short on plot, there are some interesting ideas, including a fantastically automated whore house. (Nebula nominee 1968.)

159. Silverberg, Robert, *Thorns.* A spaceman has been changed into something non-human by alien bio-engineers. A girl has "conceived" hundreds of children through biological techniques. A third person, Duncan Chalk, tries for his own amusement to manipulate the spaceman and the girl so that they will fall in love and then come to hate each other. (Hugo nominee 1968, Nebula nominee 1967.)

160. Silverberg, Robert, *Tower of Glass.* Industrialist Simeon Krug builds a great transmitter to contact a race from another star. Krug's society is peopled with humans, androids, and ectogenes—bottle-born humans. These groups' relations with each other, and the technology of the transmitter (the tower of glass), form the major interests in the story. (Nebula nominee 1970, Hugo nominee 1971.)

161. Silverberg, Robert, *Up the Line.* Jud Elliott becomes a member of the Time Service and takes up a life as a tour guide for people who want to visit the great events of the past. The story relates a series of his adventures on this job.

Several interesting time paradoxes are introduced, and little historical vignettes flesh out the plot. The story has a lot of color but drags towards the end. (Nebula nominee 1969, Hugo nominee 1970.)

162. Simak, Clifford, *All Flesh Is Grass.** A kind of group intelligence (whose individual parts are purple flowers) has broken through from a parallel universe and clamped a force field over a town, trapping the residents inside, in preparation for taking over all of Earth. The townspeople, of course, fight to save the world. (Nebula nominee 1965.)

163. Simak, Clifford, *City.** A related collection of stories about the Webster family and their Dogs and robots, followed through 10,000 years of history. The stories are told by the Dogs, who have evolved into intelligent beings. An all time favorite. (Winner of the International Fantasy Award 1953.)

164. Simak, Clifford, *Goblin Reservation.** A man is sent back to Earth by matter transmitter, but a malfunction of the equipment causes two copies of him to arrive. One copy is killed and the other copy runs into difficulty in trying to establish a rightful claim to his job and property. A strange assortment of characters, including a Neanderthal man and a ghost, try to help him out. (Hugo nominee 1969.)

165. Simak, Clifford, *They Walked Like Men.** This is an Earth-invaded-by-aliens story. The invaders are shaped like bowling balls in their natural state but can take on other shapes as suits their needs. Newspaperman Parker Graves discovers that the surreptitious invasion is underway through a series of occurrences, one of which is that huge chunks of property are being mysteriously bought up.

166. Simak, Clifford, *Time and Again.** Humans and androids struggle through time to control the

writing of a book (by Galactic agent Asher Sutton, a superman type) which will have a profound influence on the superiority of the humans over the androids (who have learned to reproduce themselves).

167. Simak, Clifford, *Way Station.** A Civil War veteran's home is converted into a matter transmitter/receiver for a Galactic civilization with the veteran as custodian. Over the years, he meets many strange creatures and finally becomes the focus of attention of the CIA. His problems are compounded by the fact that his neighbors are also becoming unfriendly and a political crisis in the galactic community is afoot. (Hugo winner 1964.)

168. Smith, Cordwainer (pen name of Paul Linebarger), *The Planet Buyer.** This story is one of the longer ones in Smith's series of stories about a far-flung and fantastic galactic culture. A fabulously rich boy buys Old Earth and goes there to enjoy his purchase. But the hero is a non-normal, and the Instrumentalities set out to trap him. (Hugo nominee 1956.)

169. Smith, George O., *The Fourth "R"** (*The Brain Machine*).* A five-year-old boy is crammed full of knowledge by his parents through a machine they invented. They are murdered, the boy wrecks the machine, and the murderer tries to get the boy to tell him its secret. The bulk of the story concerns the boy's efforts to catch the murderer and find a place for himself in the world.

170. Smith, George O., *Highways in Hiding.* Telepathy and other Psi powers are commonplace in Steve Cornell's America. But not-so-common things are happening. People mysteriously disappear, and Steve discovers strange road signs along highways, signs which seem to indicate some sort of underground organiza-

tion is at work. His investigation leads to the discovery of two competing secret groups of Mekstroms (humans who obtain superman-like powers as a result of being cured of Mekstrom's Disease).

171. Spinrad, Norman, *Bug Jack Barron.** Jack Barron is a TV personality who has a show on which he invites viewers to call in and bug him with their complaints so that he can in turn bug those people responsible for the conditions being complained about. One of his callers leads Barron into an investigation of the activities of a multi-millionaire who is eventually discovered to be committing all sorts of crimes to achieve immortality through medical technology. (Nebula nominee 1969, Hugo nominee 1970.)

172. Stapleton, Olaf, *Odd John.* Odd John is an early example of Homo-Superior. His intellectual brilliance extends to making money with his inventions. He discovers other people like himself with whom he founds a remote island colony. The group works to advance scientific knowledge and to develop new social patterns. The world discovers and assaults the colony which destroys itself. The book contains considerable characterization, with an emphasis on interpersonal relations. A classic on the superman theme.

173. Sturgeon, Theodore, *The Cosmic Rape.** An alien species, in which each individual is part of a mass intellect, moves into an Earthman's body, expecting through him to take over all of humanity. The alien hive mind is perplexed by the strangely individualistic humans but forges ahead with its plans to conquer Earth anyway.

174. Sturgeon, Theodore, *The Dreaming Jewels* (*The Synthetic Man*).* Crystalline-like aliens live among humans on Earth. Their mating dreams

produce copies of Earth objects. An embittered medical student discovers and exploits the crystals, causing them to produce freaks which he exhibits in a carnival. The freaks yearn to become part of humanity. Eventually they turn against their creator. In spite of a rather weak plot, the book has appeal because of the charisma of the characters who long to be human.

175. Sturgeon, Theodore, *More Than Human.** A group of mutant children band together to combine their different talents into something much more than ordinarily human. Their treatment at the hands of normals and their development into a new entity form a compelling story. (Each child has a different talent which enables him to play a special role in the group analogous to a part in the human body.) Another all-time favorite. (International Fantasy Award winner 1954.)

176. Sturgeon, Theodore, *Venus Plus X.** Charlie Johns wakes up to find himself in a strange city of tomorrow peopled by a unisexual race of kind and peace-loving humans. He lives among them for a time. Eventually he learns part of the secret of their creation. When he tries to return to his own world, he discovers more surprises. (Hugo nominee 1961.)

177. Tucker, Wilson, *The Long Loud Silence.** The Eastern U.S. has been nearly wiped out by biological warfare. The surviving western two-thirds cordons off the contaminated East. Corporal Russell Gary, a survivor in the East, struggles to escape into the West. Gary is a ruthless and unheroic protagonist.

178. Tucker, Wilson, *Wild Talent (Man From Tomorrow).** Paul Breen has telepathic powers. The FBI finds out about it and soon he's being used as a contact man for CIA agents behind the Iron Curtain. He's held as a virtual pris-

oner by the CIA which presents him with as
many problems as does the enemy side.

179. Tucker, Wilson, *Year of the Quiet Sun.** Brian
Chaney, a demographer and biblical scholar,
is recruited to go on an expedition into the
future in a time device built by the U.S. Bu-
reau of Standards. He and his companions,
Major Moresby and Commander Saltus, go
forward individually to different times close to
the year 2000. They find a future America
much changed from the one they know. (Nebula nominee 1970, Hugo nominee 1971.)

180. Vance, Jack, *The Dragon Masters*. A short novel
about Basics and men who have bred each
other's captives into specialized slave classes
and who are engaged in a war on a distant
planet far in the future. (Hugo winner for
short fiction 1963.)

181. Van Vogt, A. E., *Slan.** Mutant "slans", humanoids with tendrils on their heads and special Psi
powers, struggle against ordinary humans and
tendril-less slans who are trying to destroy
them. Slan youngster Jommy Cross finds he
needs to solve several puzzles in order to
emerge victorious, including the discovery of
an atomic gun invented by his father and the
location of an underground city built by true
slans centuries before.

182. Van Vogt, A. E. *The Weapon Shops of Isher.**
Weapon Shops, where any citizen can buy
a weapon, are immune from control by
the rulers of Isher. They provide the common
man with some measure of protection from
the totalitarian government. The story contains the not uncommon idea of a permanent
underground existing in opposition to the totalitarian government.

183. Vidal, Gore, *Messiah.** The story of the growth of
a theocracy which overwhelms the govern-
ments of both Christian and Communist

countries. The story is told by one of the characters who is in on the movement from the beginning. Modern advertising techniques are used to create and promulgate the "messiah's" image.

184. Vonnegut, Kurt, Jr., *Cat's Cradle.** It's a little difficult to give a coherent summary of this satirical novel. A journalist sets out to write a book about the activities of certain people on the day Hiroshima was A-bombed. At the end of the book he has become the president of a banana republic and a convert to the religion of Bokononism. Then the Earth is destroyed. (Hugo nominee 1964.)

185. Vonnegut, Kurt, Jr., *Player Piano.** The Ilium Works is the only electrical industry in the country. Since the early part of WW III it has been completely automated. Dr. Paul Proteus, a member of the executive class, is up for a big promotion. The book is concerned with satirizing certain aspects of the revolution in automation, Proteus' feelings about it, and his position in the society. (International Fantasy Award nominee 1953.)

186. Vonnegut, Kurt, Jr. *The Sirens of Titan.** Winston Niles Rumfoord exists in various times and places—at the same time. He lives on Earth, Mars, and Titan simultaneously. The plot is similarly tangled. (Hugo nominee 1960.)

187. Vonnegut, Kurt, Jr. *Slaughterhouse Five.** After receiving a concussion in an airplane crash, Billy Pilgrim becomes temporally disoriented, his consciousness shuttling back and forth along the span of his life. His experiences range from firebombing of Dresden in WW II, where he took shelter in the meatlocker of a slaughterhouse, to his assassination in Chicago in 1976. (Nebula nominee, 1969, Hugo nominee 1970.)

188. White, James, *Hospital Station.** Sector General

is a huge hospital, located between the Milky Way and the Greater Magellanic Cloud, which is staffed by a fantastic group of medicos and their equally fantastic group of patients. The book relates the solutions to a series of ingenious alien medical puzzles. (Sequel: *Star Surgeon.**)

189. Wilhelm, Kate, *The Killer Thing.* A powerful robot sets out on a rampage across the galaxy. Told in flashbacks, the story shows how the robot's drive to survive at the expense of its human creators causes it to hunt down and destroy every member of a task force sent to stop it. The story of the destruction of the robot is an allegory for the destruction of mankind itself.

190. Williamson, Jack, *The Humanoids.** A scientist creates some robots (in human form) and gives them the task of serving men and guarding them from harm. The robots do their job too well. Their helpful protection turns men into slaves. The protagonist and others try to find a way of changing the robots' instructions and ending their benevolent tyranny.

191. Wolfe, Bernard, *Limbo.* Following WW III between the U.S. and Russia, the remnants of the countries evolve the concept that man's aggressiveness can be defeated by voluntarily submitting to amputation of arms and legs. The practice is widespread. It leads to development of ingenious prosthetic devices which, of course, enable men to be as aggressive as they ever were.

192. Wyndham, John, *The Day of the Triffids.** Mankind becomes blind overnight. Triffids (large plants) come from space and infest the Earth, threatening men with extinction. (International Fantasy Award nominee 1952.)

193. Wyndham, John, *The Midwich Cuckoos.** Aliens implant their offspring in the wombs of the

women of the village of Midwich. The children look normal (except for their golden eyes), but . . . they aren't. Basis of a 1960 motion picture, *Village of the Damned*.

194. Wyndham, John, *Out of the Deeps*.* Fireballs plunge into the ocean's depths. Soon, ships begin to disappear, shorelines are raided for food (i.e., humans) and the seas begin to rise. Another of Wyndham's well done alien monster plots.

195. Wyndham, John, *Re-Birth*.* A final atomic war has caused civilization to regress to a new rural age of superstition, where a radioactively caused mutation is a sufficient reason for a child to be cast out of a community to fend for itself in the "Fringes." Some children's mutations are not physical, but mental. They form a secret society among themselves in their village. Eventually they too are forced to run for their lives.

196. Wyndham, John, *Trouble with Lichen*.* A longevity substance is discovered in a species of lichen by two scientists independently of each other. The one hides his discovery for fear of the social disruption it could cause. The other turns it into a money-making proposition. Eventually the secret does get out, and problems are created.

197. Zelazny, Roger, *Damnation Alley*.* An atomic holocaust has reduced large areas of the world to irradiated rubble. High velocity winds circle the globe, making air travel impossible. Hell Tanner, a murderer and motorcycle gang member, is promised a full pardon if he will run some plague serum across the seared continent from California to Boston, the only two remaining bits of civilization left in North America. (Short version Hugo nominee 1968.)

198. Zelazny, Roger, *Isle of the Dead*.* A number of

humans and other creatures have developed great mental powers, immortality, and wealth to the extent that they can reshape or even create whole planets. They come to think of themselves as gods and eventually engage in feuds with one another. (Nebula nominee 1969.)

199. Zelazny, Roger, *Lord of Light.** Take the great gods of Hindu and Buddhist mythology, add alien energy creatures and an elite class of humans who employ technology and Psi powers to immortalize themselves and subjugate their followers, mix well with war and intrigue, and you have Zelazny at his best. (Hugo winner 1968, Nebula nominee 1967.)

200. Zelazny, Roger, *This Immortal.** Conrad Nimikos is the mysterious hero of this story. He has apparently lived for many hundreds of years and is known by many different names. The plot concerns a political struggle between Vegans and Earthmen who have migrated from a partially destroyed Earth to a planet in the Vegan system. The value of the story lies in the author's characterization and expressive style. (Hugo winner 1966, Nebula nominee 1966.)

SUPPLEMENTARY BOOKS

This list includes books which do not fit in the first category, but which should not go unmentioned. The list is divided into categories as indicated.

SINGLE AUTHOR COLLECTIONS
For the most part, books are listed here because (1) the author's significant contribution to the field has been greater in the area of short fiction than long, or (2) omission of the stories in the collections would reduce the quality of our recommendations.

Aldiss, Brian, *The Long Afternoon of Earth.**

Asimov, Isaac, *I Robot,** *The Rest of the Robots,** Earth *Is Room Enough.*

Beaumont, Charles, *The Hunger and Other Stories.*

Blish, James, *The Seedling Stars.*

Bradbury, Ray, *The Illustrated Man,** *The Golden Apples of the Sun,** Dandelion Wine.*

Brown, Frederic, *Angels and Spaceships, Space on My Hands.*

Campbell, John W., Jr., *Who Goes There?, The Cloak of Aesir.*

Clarke, Arthur C., *Reach for Tomorrow, Tales of Ten Worlds,** Expedition to Earth.**

Collier, John, *Fancies and Goodnights.*

Davidson, Avram, *Or All the Seas with Oysters.*

DeCamp, L. Sprague, *The Wheels of If.* *

Ellison, Harlan, *I Have No Mouth and I Must Scream.*

Farmer, Philip Jose, *Strange Relations.*

Finney, Jack, *The Third Level.*

Heinlein, Robert, *The Man Who Sold the Moon,* * *The Green Hills of Earth,* * *The Menace from Earth.* *

Knight, Damon, *Far Out.*

Kornbluth, Cyril, *The Marching Morons, A Mile Beyond the Moon.*

Niven, Larry, *Neutron Star.* *

Oliver, Chad, *Another Kind.*

Russell, Eric Frank, *Deep Space.*

Sheckley, Robert, *Untouched by Human Hands, Pilgrimage to Earth.*

Smith, Cordwainer, *Space Lords.* *

Sturgeon, Theodore, *A Touch of Strange,* * *Caviar,* * *Without Sorcery.*

Tenn, William, *The Human Angle.*

Weinbaum, Stanley, *A Martian Odyssey.* *

Wyndham, John, et al., *Sometime Never.*

Zelazny, Roger, *Four For Tomorrow.*

ANTHOLOGIES
Anthologies abound in science fiction. Some people (e.g., the late Groff Conklin) have made names for themselves within the field by editing them. Many anthologies are built around common subject themes (e.g., telepathy). Others may belong to a series, with a new volume added to the series annually. Some stories are so popular that they have been anthologized several times. Our recommendations are listed below, by editor.

Amis, Kingsley, and Conquest, Robert, *Spectrum, Spectrum II,** etc.

Asimov, Isaac, *The Hugo Winners* (Vol. I and Vol. II).

Boucher, Anthony, *A Treasury of Great Science Fiction* (2 volumes).

Boucher, Anthony, and McComas, Francis; or Mills, Robert, *The Best from Fantasy and Science Fiction.* This series began in 1956, and represents the editors' choices. In later years, Mills took over the job from Boucher and McComas.

Campbell, John W., Jr., *The Astounding Science Fiction Anthology.* Selected by editor Campbell from his magazine *Astounding Science Fiction;* not a series.

Conklin, Groff, *Thirteen Great Stories of Science Fiction,** *Great Stories of Space Travel,** *Invaders of Earth.*

Ellison, Harlan, *Dangerous Visions.**

Healy, Raymond, and McComas, Francis, *Adventures in Time and Space.*

Knight, Damon, *A Century of Great Science Fiction, Orbit 1, Orbit 2,* etc.

Merril, Judith, *The Year's Greatest SF.* This series began in 1956.

Mills, Robert, *A Decade of Fantasy and Science Fiction.* A "summary" of the Boucher-McComas/Mills series listed above.

Pohl, Frederik, *Star of Stars.* A summary of Pohl's series *Star Science Fiction 1-6.*

Serling, Rod, *Stories from the Twilight Zone.**

Silverberg, Robert, *The Science Fiction Hall of Fame.*

SERIES

Series of novel length stories are common in science fiction, and several of them have been noted in the main list. We list five series here because there is no other appropriate place for them and because these particular books seem to have a special attraction for teenage readers.

Burroughs, Edgar Rice,
The Venus Series, e.g., *Pirates of Venus,* Lost on Venus,* Carson on Venus,* Escape on Venus.**
The Mars Series, e.g., *A Princess of Mars,* The Gods of Mars,* The Warlord of Mars,* Thuvia, Maid of Mars,* Fighting Man of Mars,* Swords of Mars,* Synthetic Men of Mars,* John Carter of Mars.**

Howard, Robert E.,
The Conan Series, e.g., *Conan the Adventurer,* Conan the Freebooter, Conan, Conan the Warrior,* Conan the Usurper,* Conan the Conqueror,* Conan the Avenger,* Conan of the Isles.*
This series was later supplemented with stories by L. Sprague De Camp and Lin Carter who had access to Howard's notes on unfinished stories and were themselves competent writers of the same kind of stories. Some of the titles listed above are by them.

Smith, E. E. ("Doc"),
The Skylark Series, e.g. *Skylark of Space,* Skylark Three,* Skylark of Valeron,* Skylark DuQuesne.**
The Lensman Series, e.g., *Triplanetary, First Lensman, Children of the Lens, Masters of the Vortex.*

FANTASY
The line between science fiction and fantasy is not always sharp. Many writers write both kinds of stories. Here, we have listed a few fantasies which we think students will particularly enjoy.

Anderson, Poul, *Three Hearts and Three Lions.**

DeCamp, L. Sprague, and Pratt, Fletcher, *The Incomplete Enchanter*. This is one of several books of magic *cum* parallel universe themes by these two authors.

Jackson, Shirley, *The Haunting of Hill House.**

Swann, Thomas Burnett, *The Day of the Minotaur*.

Tolkien, J. R. R., *The Lord of the Rings Trilogy*. This monumental work has so endeared itself to readers that a whole cult has sprung up around it.

POTPOURRI
The books listed below do not fit into our main list for one reason or another, and so they are listed here. A number of the books mentioned in the introductory essay should be thought of as belonging to this list.

Capek, Karel, *R.U.R.*

Doyle, Arthur Conan, *The Lost World*.

Lewis, C. S., Trilogy: *That Hideous Strength, Perelandra, Out of the Silent Planet*.

Priestley, J. B., *The Doomsday Men*.

Sheil, M. P., *The Purple Cloud*.

Shute, Nevil, *On the Beach*.*

Skinner, B. F., *Walden Two*.*

Stapleton, Olaf, *To the End of Time*.

Verne, Jules, *Twenty Thousand Leagues Under the Sea*,* *Journey to the Center of the Earth*.*

Wells, H. G., *Seven Famous Novels*.

Wright, S. Fowler, *The Throne of Saturn*.

Wylie, Philip, and Balmer, Edwin, *When Worlds Collide*,* *After Worlds Collide*.*

The End